Illusion or Opportunity

Illusion or Opportunity

Civil Society and the Quest for Social Change

Henry Veltmeyer

Fernwood Publishing • Halifax

Editing: Brenda Conroy
Cover Art: Erica Veltmeyer
Printed and bound in Canada by Hignell Book Printing

Published in Canada by Fernwood Publishing
Site 2A, Box 5, 32 Oceanvista Lane
Black Point, Nova Scotia, B0J 1B0
and 324 Clare Avenue, Winnipeg, Manitoba, R3L 1S3
www.fernwoodpublishing.ca

Fernwood Publishing Company Limited gratefully acknowledges the financial support
of the Government of Canada through the Book Publishing Industry Development
Program (BPDIP), the Canada Council for the Arts and the Nova Scotia
Department of Tourism and Culture for our publishing program.

Library and Archives Canada Cataloguing in Publication

Veltmeyer, Henry
Illusion or opportunity: civil society and the quest for social
change / Henry Veltmeyer.

Includes bibliographical references and index.
ISBN 978-1-55266-230-4

1. Economic development--Social aspects. 2. Civil society.
3. Social change. 4. Social policy--Economic aspects. 5. Community
development. I. Title.

HM831.V45 2006   338.9   C2006-906689-2

Contents

Introduction

It has been argued that the idea of "development" was constructed as part of a plan to rescue economically backward (and politically wayward) decolonized countries from the lure of communism and to steer them along a capitalist and democratic path. Development, a project advanced with cooperation by diverse agencies and governments in the wealthy North, began to take the same form that it had in the already developed West, namely economic growth, industrialization, modernization and capitalism. However, in the late 1970s, the entire project was seemingly derailed, bedevilled by problems arising out of a global economic crisis, a relative failure to bring about significant improvements in the "developing countries" and growing pressures for revolutionary change. These problems in turn gave rise to ideas and actions in the direction of a solution to the crisis.

One widely adopted strategy was technological conversion: applying new information and other technologies to the economic production apparatus of the world capitalist system. Another solution was to establish a "new world order" in which the factors of production (investment capital and trade in goods and services) were liberated from the constraints of government regulation, creating a world in which the "forces of freedom, liberty and private enterprise" could flourish. Another approach was to change the way that development was conceived and put into practice.

This latter approach has given rise to a worldwide movement in the direction of "another development" — a form that is integral (social as well as economic), oriented towards meeting people's basic needs, people-centred and initiated from below, human in scale and form, equitable and socially more inclusive (of women, indigenous communities, etc.), capacitating and empowering of the poor, sustainable in terms of the environment and livelihoods, participatory and community-based.

This idea of "another development" is a major theme in this book, which includes a series of analytical probes into the dynamics of social change — its theory and practice. Chapter 1 briefly traces the evolution of this idea, thereby establishing a context for questions raised and discussed in subsequent chapters. The chapter also reviews ideas associated with other ways of understanding the dynamics of social change in a contemporary context: the terms "development," "globalization" and "imperialism" constitute alternative reference points for understanding the social change dynamics of the new world order. These concepts and the dynamics reviewed in Chapter 1 also provide a backdrop for the probes into the dynamics of social change discussed in the book.

Chapter 2 reconstructs the thinking of an international organization and financial institution, the World Bank, *vis-à-vis* the idea of development, which it views as a response to world poverty, the conditions of which afflict up to two-fifths of humankind. The World Bank has assumed a leading role in the five-decade-long war on world poverty, which the Bank sees as the major obstacle to the historic march towards progress in which countries and organizations across the world are engaged. The chapter explores — and critically assesses — the Bank's thinking about this problem and reconstructs the strategic permutations of the war waged against world poverty by the Bank and its strategic partners in the international development community. The chapter also identifies the reasons why this war has been such a dismal failure — why five decades of concerted efforts and campaigns by armies of intergovernmental and nongovernmental organizations have failed to win the war, despite the expenditure of enormous financial and human resources.

The thinking and the practice of the World Bank and its strategic partners in this war on poverty have changed over the years — and yet they have not. Chapter 3 examines the latest twist in the development project: the new paradigm of social capital and local development. The thinking and practice associated with this new paradigm are critically analyzed and assessed as to its outcomes and prospects for alleviating poverty and bringing about an improvement in peoples' lives and a sustainable form of economic and social development.

The structural adjustment to the requirements of the new world order, a process that has unfolded over the course of the last two decades, has both an economic and a political dimension. In economic terms this process entails the integration of societies across the world into a global economy that has been restructured so as to release the forces of economic freedom. This restructuring process has brought about a dramatic change in the institutions and role of the market and the state, strengthening the former and weakening the latter. The political dimension to this restructuring process, and the shift from a state-led to a market-friendly form of economic and social development, relates to the need to restore political order under conditions of a transition from one world order to another.

Chapter 4 examines the dynamics of this transition. The process of structural adjustment and globalization associated with this transition generated new forms of social exclusion, poverty and inequality (see Chapter 2), which in turn spawned new forms of political resistance that threaten the existing political order and that have made many societies and economies difficult to govern or ungovernable. The result has been a political process directed towards new forms of governance — for restoring order. Since "government" in the emerging and now dominant neoliberal worldview and economic model is viewed as "bad," very much part of the problem needing redress, the search for "good governance" has been directed towards "civil society," democratizing its relation to the state and actively engaging a process of participatory development and politics. The chapter reconstructs the thinking behind this process.

Poverty and development in their diverse dimensions, and the dynamics of social change, can be viewed and analyzed in both rural and urban contexts. Chapter 5 analyzes these dynamics in the context of rural society in Latin America. Poverty in this context has been and is viewed by the World Bank and other agencies involved in the development project as a matter of "social exclusion," which can best be addressed by combining a supportive policy framework with a process of local development based on "self-help" and the agency of grassroots and nongovernmental organizations within civil society. The dominant response of the rural poor (the peasantry, landless workers and indigenous communities) in Latin America and elsewhere has been to confront the holders and the structure of economic and political power with the demand for social change, and to press this demand in the form of direct action — mobilizing the forces of resistance against the economic model used to make economic and social policy.

Chapter 5 explores the diverse permutations of this social-movements approach towards social change in the context of efforts by governments, international financial institutions such as the World Bank and development agencies to provide the rural poor an alternative path. In this context, development, particularly in the form of financing local micro-projects, is presented as a viable alternative to the social mobilization of the forces of opposition to the state. The option presented to the rural poor is either to persist with the confrontational and "revolutionary" approach favoured by the social movements or to take the less divisive and more fruitful approach promoted by the World Bank and its partners: local development based on self-help, empowerment and the accumulation of social capital.

Chapter 6 explores in general terms the modalities of social change that dominate and continue to characterize the political landscape in Latin America and elsewhere in the new world order. In the 1960s, in the wake of the Cuban revolution and fears of another Cuba, the path to social change was paved with state power. Social change was to be accomplished by challenging the political class and capturing the state apparatus, the major repository of political power. This could be done either by means of the democratic electoral process — the parliamentary road — or through mass mobilization of the insurrectionary forces of resistance — the revolutionary path. In the 1960s and 1970s this political option was expressed in the maxim: reform

3

or revolution. Today, the political option continues to define the agenda of the popular movement. But added to the political mix is the "no-power" option: to bring about social change, not by challenging or confronting the power structure but by working within the local spaces of this structure.

Chapter 6 reviews recent political developments associated with the dynamics of social change in the context of Argentina, Bolivia, Brazil and Ecuador, countries that exemplify the political dynamics associated with the state-power and no-power approaches. The book concludes with an assessment of the prospects of the forces of opposition and resistance to neoliberalism and capitalist development in bringing about social change and paving an alternative road towards socialism.

Chapter 1

The Macrodynamics of Social Change

The epoch-defining changes of recent decades can be understood in three different ways. One is as "development," a project initiated immediately after the Second World War but which, after the onset of a systemwide economic crisis in the 1970s and a theoretical impasse in the 1980s, has been reborn in the shape of a new paradigm — social change initiated from below and within civil society rather than from above and outside. Another understanding of the macrodynamics of transformative social change makes reference to "globalization" as a process designed to promote "a single sustainable model for national success: freedom, democracy and private enterprise" — to quote George W. Bush (2002). In this approach the transformative social changes that have characterized world developments in recent years are viewed as the irresistible and desirable outcome of economic and political adjustments to the requirements of a new world order, a process in which — to return to George W. Bush — "good" (the forces of economic and political freedom, prosperity and peace) will vanquish "evil" (constraints on these forces, opponents of freedom, rogue regimes). A third way of understanding these changes and associated developments is as "imperialism," that is, the drive for world domination and the subordination of social and economic development to the hegemonic power of a global empire. In fact, it is argued that both development and globalization can be understood as imperialism, different faces of the same project of world domination and longstanding efforts of the United States to establish its hegemony over the whole system.

As for the dynamics of social change, the argument of this chapter is in three parts. Part I reconstructs some of the major macroeconomic dynamics of international development, conceived as a "strategic (geopolitical, foreign policy) project" and as an "objective process" of nation-building and economic progress. It is argued that international cooperation for international development, in both its bilateral and multilateral forms, was designed as a means of ensuring that postcolonial states in their pursuit of national development would not succumb to the lure of communism and the model presented by the Soviet Union. Teresa Hayter (1971) in this context defined "aid" as imperialism, i.e., it is one of several available and constructed means of advancing the foreign policy and economic interests of the U.S. and its allies.

Part II turns towards the discourse on globalization, presented by the

World Bank and its strategic partners in the international development and finance community as a form of development (a means of stimulating economic growth). Although the discourse on globalization captures some important macrodynamics of social change, I argue that globalization is little more than a mask for the imperial dream of world domination; that imperialism provides a better descriptor of social change — of conditions that can be identified at the national level.

Part III summarizes some of the critical dimensions of imperialism, the project to advance the geopolitical and economic interests of the U.S. in any and every way possible. I assert that U.S. imperialism, both in regard to the projection of military power and in the form of development and globalization, provides the context for the emergence and spread of a multifaceted popular movement that is global in its connections if not in scale. This movement embodies diverse forces of resistance and organizations for social change.

The chapter ends on this point, concluding that nongovernmental development organizations and other elements of civil society have been pressed into imperial service, providing strategic assistance to the empire in its concern and effort to quell the fire of revolutionary ferment on the southern periphery of the world system, particularly in the countryside of rural development and social movements.

Development as Imperialism

Although it can be traced back to the eighteenth-century Enlightenment and the idea of progress, development as we know it (as a macro-project involving, or based on, international cooperation) had its birth in U.S. foreign policy and the Cold War — in efforts orchestrated by the U.S. State Department to ensure that the postcolonial state in the economically "backward" areas of the developing world would not follow the example for rapid growth and national development set by the U.S.S.R.

The 1940–1950s: Foreign Aid and the War against Communism

According to Wolfgang Sachs (1992) and his associates in "postdevelopment theory" (Esteva and Prakash, 1998), development was invented in the late 1940s as a form of imperialism — a means of imposing relations of domination on peoples and states struggling to liberate themselves from the yoke of colonialism. The idea of development is here traced back to the Point-Four Program of overseas development assistance (ODA) announced by U.S. President Truman on January 10, 1949. In its multilateral form it originates in projects funded by the International Bank of Reconstruction and Development (subsequently known as the World Bank) in Chile in 1948 and in Brazil and Mexico the year after. The World Bank is a pillar of the

6

Bretton Woods system, designed to resurrect the global form of capitalist development and international trade (and international economic integration) characteristic of earlier epochs.

The U.S. government was by far the major donor of ODA, and the foreign policy geopolitical and strategic considerations of the U.S. government were the most relevant in shaping the form that it would take. From the beginning there existed an extensive internal policy debate as to the possible uses of foreign aid. The central issue had to do with how it could serve the U.S.'s broader geopolitical strategic interests. Some voices claimed that it would not be in the economic interest of the U.S. to promote economic development in the backward areas of the world and that efforts to contain the underdeveloped countries within the western bloc would be unrealistic and not fruitful. But the view prevailed that ODA was indeed a useful means of advancing the geopolitical interests of the U.S. (to prevent the spread of communism) without damaging its economic interests (Cohen, 1968).

The 1960s and 1970s: The Dynamics of Reform versus Revolution

In the developing world, the emphasis of foreign aid was on building the administrative capacity of the state and providing infrastructure for both public and private enterprise — "nation-building" in the parlance of imperial policy. In Latin America, however, as well as in parts of Asia, the main concern was to stave off pressures for revolutionary change — to prevent another Cuba (and China). To this end the United States Agency for International Development (USAID) promoted state-led reforms and public provision of credit and technical assistance to the rural poor.

Much of ODA took a bilateral form (government to government) but USAID also turned to nongovernmental organizations (NGOs) to channel funds more directly to local communities. These NGOs ("private voluntary organizations," as they were termed) not only provided a useful channel for ODA but also for collateral services of benefit to donors, such as the strengthening of local organizations that were opting for social reform and local development rather than social revolution and the weakening of class-based anti-systemic/anti-capitalist state organizations. In this context, NGOs were also used — somewhat innocently from the perspective of their middle-class workers — not only to elude revolution and promote economic and social development but to promote the virtues of democracy and capitalism — the use of the electoral mechanism in politics, the market mechanism (free trade, mobile capital) in economics and reform as the modality of change.

In effect, as noted by Bombarolo, Coscio Perez and Stein (1990) and argued by Petras (in Petras and Veltmeyer, 2001), many if not most NGOs have tended to serve as executing agents of U.S. imperialism, promoting values and behaviour functional for the economic and political interests of the growing U.S. empire. In this they resembled the missionaries of the old imperialism, who promoted change in the next rather than this world; in this case, they spread the good word about reform and democracy — and information about the evil forces (communism, revolutionary change) that were lurking in the land.

The difference between the new missionaries and the missionaries of old — then again perhaps there is no fundamental difference — is that more often than not they were unaware of the broader implications of their interventions. Generally they were — as they are today — composed of well-intentioned individuals concerned to make a difference, albeit small, in the lives of people they touched with their assistance. Nevertheless, in their micro-projects and mediations between the donors and recipient organizations, they could not help but promote an alternative to the politics of revolutionary change — and it was to this end that they were contracted and funded. USAID and the broader donor community used NGOs as partners in the shared development enterprise. They helped turn local communities away from revolution and toward reform and, in the process, created conditions that would allow the empire to advance its economic and geopolitical interests.

Foreign Aid in a System in Transition, 1973–1983
The years 1948–1973 have been described as the golden age of capitalism (Marglin and Schor, 1990). But in the late 1960s, cracks began to appear in the foundations of the system. The result was an extended period of crisis and efforts to restructure the system as a way out. One strategic response involved a direct assault on labour by capital, which attacked labour's share of national income, to that point linked to productivity gains, its organizational capacity and political power (Crouch and Pizzorno, 1978; Davis, 1984; Tabb, 2004). The aim of this counteroffensive was to increase the pool of capital available for productive investment. The result was a compression of wages to the point that in many cases their value or purchasing power in 2003 was still below levels achieved in 1973 (Weisbrot, Baker, Kraev and Chen, 2001). In the U.S., for example, wages fell 10 percentage points in as many years (1974–83) and continued to fall, particularly in the years of Reaganomics, in which the individuals in the upper reaches (the top one percent) of the wealth and income hierarchy appropriated all of the proceeds of economic growth. In Latin America, the power of organized labour regarding the capacity to negotiate collective agreements for higher wages and improved conditions was so reduced that the share of labour (wages and salaries) in national income (and value added to production) in many cases fell by half — from over 40 percent in the 1970s to below 20 percent after a decade and more of neoliberal reform. This process of income concentration and associated conditions of wealth and poverty on the extremes of income distribution unfolded on a global scale, but in some countries and regions the results were particularly dramatic. In Argentina, for example, even today, after more than

a decade of economic restructuring and neoliberal reform, the level of per capita income is still well below that achieved in 1970. And Argentina is by no means an isolated or the most exemplary case.

Other less direct strategic responses to the worldwide capitalist crisis included a process of technological conversion and productive transformation; the evolution of a new more flexible form of regulation — postFordism; a global restructuring of finance, provided primarily in the form of "official" ODA, which at the time dominated global North-South capital flows ("international transfer of resources" in official discourse); and a restructuring of national macroeconomic policy on the basis of what the World Bank economists dubbed the "structural adjustment."

Regarding financial capital flows the dominant stream took the form of ODA, offered as supplemental finance to stimulate economic growth. Until 1983 such official transfers of financial resources were channelled into projects designed to establish the infrastructure for economic activity and nation-building. However, after the onset of a regionwide debt crisis, official transfers began to assume a different form — loans conditioned by policy reforms oriented towards the free market and democracy (Burnside and Dollar, 1997; Carothers, 1999; Rodrik, 1995). Until this point the World Bank and other international financial institutions (IFIs) had taken the position that ODA would service development strategies that were "owned" by countries pursuing their own development path. But with the leverage provided by the debt crisis, bank lending was conditional on structural reforms designed by economists at the World Bank — reforms that were market friendly and conducive to "good governance" (Kaufmann, Kraay and Zoido-Lobatón, 1999; World Bank, 1994).

In the wake of the global production crisis in the early 1970s, U.S. and European commercial banks had initiated a lending policy that led to an explosion of private capital and debt financing. The flows involved in this form of capital would come to exceed the official resource transfers (ODA) and, for some years (particularly in the first half of the 1990s), the flow of capital associated with multinational corporations (MNCs). Table 1.1 provides a historical picture of these capital flows as well as some of the returns on them.

The data in Table 1.1 reflect global trends in international resource transfers, including the eclipse of ODA by private capital flows; a dramatic decline of commercial lending in the 1980s and then again after the Asian financial crisis in 1997; and the growth of foreign direct investment (FDI) as the dominant flow of capital (the "backbone of private sector external financial flows," as the International Monetary Fund [IMF] puts it), used primarily to acquire the assets of privatized enterprises or merge with other firms. The data also reflect the imperial agency of the world's largest transnational

Table 1.1 Long-Term North-South Financial Flows,
1985–2001 (in USD billions)

	'85–89	'90–94	'95	'96	'97	'98	'99	'00	'01
ODA	200.0	274.6	55.3	31.2	43.0	54.5	46.1	37.9	36.2
Private	157.0	547.5	206.1	276.6	300.8	283.2	224.4	225.8	
FDI	76.0	268.5	106.8	130.8	172.5	178.3	184.4	166.7	
PI*	6.0	111.5	36.1	49.2	30.2	15.6	34.5	50.9	18.5
Other	75.0	172.5	63.2	126.2	98.1	-10.7	25.5	8.2	-26.7
Net Resource Inflow	357.0	822.5	261.4	307.8	343.8	337.7	270.5	263.7	
FDI Profits	66.0	96.5	26.5	30.0	31.8	35.2	40.3	45.4	55.3
Debt Payments	354.0	356.5	100.8	106.6	112.9	118.7	121.9	126.7	
Net Resource Outflow	420.0	453.0	227.3	136.6	144.7	153.9	162.2	172.1	

Source: World Bank (2002). * PI = portfolio investment

corporations, the basic operating units of the U.S. empire, whose operations in Latin America alone — facilitated by a process of financial liberalization — netted over USD100 billion in profits in the 1990s (Saxe-Fernández and Núñez, 2001). And these net resource transfers do not take into account the surplus value extracted from the direct producers and workers through wage exploitation, relations of international trade and other means.

The Imperialism of Foreign Aid and Debt
With the onset of the debt crisis, creditors lined up behind the World Bank and the IMF and capital in the form of loans dried up. Table 1.1 suggests that in the 1980s over USD350 billion was diverted from the developing countries (primarily Latin America) to the head offices of the commercial banks — a capital drain that led directly to a "decade lost to development" in Latin America. As of 1995 virtually no new loan funds have been extended to developing countries by the commercial banks while another $800 billion were "lost to development" due to policy reforms set by the World Bank as a conditionality of further "aid" (Burnside and Dollar, 1997; Mosley, 1999; World Bank, 1998). Saxe-Fernández and Núñez (2001) documented a huge net outflow from Latin America to the American and European centres of the empire by diverse means, primarily financial mechanisms of surplus transfer. The United States Conference on Trade and Development (UNCTAD 2004) extended this study to all developing societies on the periphery of the world capitalist system.

These World Bank policy reforms and their dynamics have been subject to considerably study, particularly as regards their socioeconomic impacts (see, for example, Gwin and Nelson, 1997). They are based on what has become known as the new economic model or, more revealingly, neoliberalism, a doctrine that argues the need for countries to integrate their economies into a single global economy. These policies include privatization of public enterprises, liberalization of trade and financial flows, deregulation of product, capital and labour markets, and downsizing of the state, particularly as regards economic and social programming. The point of these structural reforms, aimed at substituting the institutions of private enterprise for the state, is to unleash the forces of economic freedom, allowing them to operate with as few constraints as possible.

The 1990s saw the global spread of a virus that first affected Mexico and then in mid-1997, Southeast Asia. By most accounts caused by the volatile and deregulated movement of hundreds of billions of dollars in capital in search of short-term profit, the "Asian crisis" devastated economy after economy in the region, stilling talk (and much writing) about the economic miracle of rapid growth in parts of Asia. The financial crisis resurrected the spectre of a more generalized economic crisis, even a collapse of the system. Under these conditions the multinational commercial banks again pulled out, leaving a vacuum only partially filled by FDI (the privatization bonanza was largely over), leading to another half decade lost to development (ECLAC, 2002). Official aid flows in this context were minimal and largely "unproductive," as were FDI flows, destined as they largely were to the purchase and acquisition of privatized assets. The results of these developments are not hard to find. They are exemplified in the experience of Argentina, hitherto the strongest economy in Latin America but now in the throes of a far-reaching crisis and in default on its debt payment obligations to its external creditors.

Alternative Development and Imperialism
in an Era of Globalization, 1983–2003

As noted, ODA originated as a policy for meeting the strategic foreign policy requirements of the U.S. state. In retrospect, it can quite properly be described as imperial policy — in the service of a long-established project of world domination and hegemony.[1] Subsequently, with the agency of the NGOs, the development project was constructed as a means of defusing pressures for revolutionary change within its client states. The history of U.S. intervention in Central America — one of the more successful arenas for the projection of U.S. state power — testifies that more often than not development did not work. True, no other Cuba emerged in the region, but this was the result not so much of the operations of USAID as the projection of military force and the extensive "aid" provided to counterinsurgency forces in the region.

In the 1980s an entirely new context was created for ODA by the neoliberal project of globalization. The development project was not abandoned but it was restructured — designed as an alternative, more participatory form of development, based on the partnership of intergovernmental and nongovernmental organizations, which would mediate between the donors and the grassroots in the execution of a new generation of projects targeted at the problem of poverty. The actual flow of funds channelled through these NGOs, many of which were unwittingly converted into agents of the new imperialism, was actually very modest (less than 10 percent of the total), but it was enough to induce many organizations in the popular sector to turn away from direct collective action against the system and to opt for a participatory form of local development.

This form of development is not predicated on the accumulation of natural, physical and financial assets but rather of "social capital," which, unlike the accumulation of other forms of capital, requires neither political confrontation with the power structure nor substantive change (Knack, 1999; Woolcock and Narayan, 2000). Rather than attempting to change the structure of power, such development aims to change how people feel about themselves. It is oriented towards "empowerment," providing the poor with a sense of participation and involvement in decision-making (albeit limited to decisions as to how to spend the meagre poverty-alleviation funds that come their way). It is in this context that Heloise Weber (2002) could write of micro-finance and micro-credit as a "coherent set of tools that may facilitate as well as govern the globalization agenda." From "the perspective of the architects of global development," she writes, "the micro-credit agenda [and thus, the poverty-alleviation strategy of the World Bank — Sustainable Banking with the Poor]... is conducive to facilitating policy changes at the local level according to the logic of globalization... while at the same time advancing its potential to discipline locally in the global governance agenda" (2002: 146).

Foreign Aid as a Catalyst of Regression
Until the 1980s, ODA was the dominant form of international resource flows. The rationale for ODA was an assumed incapacity of developing countries to accumulate sufficient capital to finance their development. The provision of supplementary finance was deemed to have a catalytic effect, generating conditions that would reduce poverty and stimulate economies to grow. However, over fifty years of experience have demonstrated that aid more likely serves the interests of the donor country and that ODA functions, as do other forms of resource flows, as a mechanism of surplus transfer, a catalyst not of development but of regression.

The evidence is clear. After two decades of rapid growth within the Bretton Woods system, the development process stalled precisely in areas subject to structural adjustment and dependence on both FDI — commercial bank lending — and ODA. Parts of the "Third World" — to be precise, a group of newly industrializing countries in East and Southeast Asia — continued to experience high rates of economic growth and with this growth a substantial improvement in social and economic conditions. However, these countries neither pursued a neoliberal strategy nor were structurally adjusted to the requirements of the new world order. In Latin America and Sub-Saharan Africa, structural reforms and ODA were (and are) associated with a decided deterioration in social economic conditions, which includes a dramatic growth in the inequality in the distribution of wealth and income and a substantial increase in the number of people living and working in conditions of abject poverty.

By the end of the 1990s, an estimated three billion people, close to 44 percent of the world's population, were identified as unable to meet their basic needs and an estimated 1.4 billion were forced to subsist on less than a dollar a day, under conditions of abject poverty. Some of this poverty is rooted in longstanding structures of social exclusion, but a large part either originates in, or is exacerbated by, the policy reforms attached to ODA. Aid can indeed be viewed as a catalyst of underdevelopment and regression rather than growth and development.

The record could not be clearer. In the neoliberal era of globalization and structural adjustment, this regression is the direct result of the policy conditions of ODA. In a brief on corporate globalization and the poor, Mokhiber and Weissman (2001) report on a study by the Center for Economic and Policy Research (CEPR). Seventy-two percent of eighty-nine countries in its survey experienced a decline in their per capita income of at least five percentage points from the 1960–1980 period, which was governed by state-led development, to 1980–2000, an era dominated by the new economic model of free market capitalism. The only developing countries that did well in the latter period were those that ignored the policy prescriptions of the IMF and the World Bank. The CEPR estimates that eighteen countries would have doubled their per capita income if they had stayed on their earlier development path.

Imperialism as Globalization
Crisis and Restructuring under the New Economic Model
One aspect of the class war unleashed by capital in the 1970s was a direct assault on labour. Another was a turn towards a new economic policy agenda based on a neoclassical economic theory that held up the world market as the fundamental engine of economic growth and the private sector enterprises (MNCs) as its driver. In the orthodoxy of development theory in the 1950s and 1960s, the absence or weakness of the capitalist class in economically backward countries required the state to step in and assume the function

of capital (investment, entrepreneurship, management) and a leading role in the economy. With reference to this idea, the pioneers of development economics designed a model that was highly functional for governments in the developing world. It emphasized the need for and resulted in a policy emphasis on (1) nationalization — state takeover of firms in strategic industries, not just in the areas of infrastructure, utilities and social programming but in leading sectors of the economy; (2) regulation of economic activity and commodity, capital and labour markets; (3) import substitution based on the protection of domestic industry from outside competition; (4) an inward orientation of national production; and (5) increased programming in the areas of economic development and social welfare.

Under conditions of a by then decade-long and system-wide production crisis, a growing fiscal crisis and an impending debt crisis, this model succumbed to attacks on it from the right, which had achieved state power in the southern cone of South America in the 1970s and managed to capture state power in the U.S., the U.K. and elsewhere in the developing and developed world. On the basis of several Latin American experiments with the "most sweeping economic reforms in history," economists at the World Bank designed a "new economic model," designed to reverse a decade-long trend towards the steady incorporation of the working class and non-capitalist producers into the economic and political development process. This model, dubbed and subsequently known as neoliberalism, prescribed a package of policies (presented as structural reforms) that make up what Williamson (1990) has termed the Washington Consensus.

The Economics of Adjustment: Globalization in Theory, Neoliberalism in Practice

The new economic model, and the policy reform program derived from it, was presented by the World Bank as a development program, i.e., as the only way of moving forward, placing countries on the path of economic growth and prosperity and, in the process, providing necessary conditions for attacking the problem of widespread poverty. However, it was clear that the agenda behind these policies was not economic development but rather globalization, the creation of a world economy based on economic freedom within the policy and institutional framework of the "new world order." The first clear reference to this agenda was in 1986, at a conference convened by the U.S. Council for Foreign Relations, a major part of the "braintrust of the system," the rulers of the world (Ostry, 1990). At this point, globalization was presented not as it would be some years later — as a *process*, i.e., as the inevitable outcome of the workings of a system that did not allow for any alternatives. It was presented as a *project* with desirable outcomes (economic growth, etc.).

The object of this consensus was to create a system in which — to paraphrase George W. Bush's 2002 national security report — the forces of economic and political freedom could flourish, vanquishing the enemies of freedom and obstacles such as government regulation, capital controls and restrictions on the movement of goods and capital. The necessary condition for this development was the structural adjustment of national economies to the requirements of this new world economic order (adoption of the specified structural "reforms" in their national policy), leading to their integration into the world economy. By the end of the decade in Latin America all but four countries were more or less integrated under conditions of privatization and financial liberalization, so much so that private capital (the IFIs and MNCs) had managed to achieve dominion over the global economy, generating an enormous influx and reflux of capital. The bulk of this capital — over 95 percent, it has been estimated — is either speculative or unproductive in nature, used to acquire privatized and other firms or to speculate on exchange rates or futures contracts rather than productive investment in new technology.

Studies by Saxe-Fernández (2002) have established some of the outcomes of the process, which, in the 1990s, was extended to Argentina, Brazil and Peru, three of the holdout countries relatively slow to get on the globalization train (but once they did they moved with alacrity and speed). The negligible economic growth and increased social inequalities in the distribution of global (and national) incomes, and conditions of poverty and wealth at the extremes of this distribution, are, of course, well known. They have been subject to considerable study, and the facts are well established, albeit with diverse interpretation. But what Saxe-Fernández established is a pronounced trend towards asset denationalization and a system that allowed the MNCs to generate an enormous pool of capital and siphon off financial resources in the form of profit on direct investments, interest on bank loans and portfolio investments and royalty payments, not to mention labour exploitation and unfair trade. According to UNCTAD (2004), taking a global view, this process in 2004 generated a net outflow of capital from the countries on the periphery of the system to the tune of USD239 billion.

*Capitalism and Democracy: A Marriage
of Convenience or Strategic Necessity?*
Before the advent of globalization, the idea held by most political scientists in the liberal tradition was that authoritarian regimes provided better conditions than democratic ones for implementing economic growth-producing policy reforms. For their part Samuel Huntington and his associates (Crozier, Huntington and Watanuki, 1975) had established the politically destabilizing effects of too much democracy, generating as it did expectations on which the system could not deliver and thus conditions of political instability. However, within the framework of the neoliberal model, the contrary idea was advanced and took root: that political liberalization and democracy

would provide better conditions for economic liberalization (Dominguez and Lowenthal, 1996; Rueschmeyer and Stephens, 1992). The idea of democracy in this context was closely tied to the aversion of neoclassical/ neoliberal economists (and the new political economy of Krueger and her associates at the World Bank and the IMF) towards government, viewing it, as Adam Smith did, as a predatory device open to corruption and giving rise to "rentierism" — the use by groups to advance their special rather than the public interest. It was also tied to the concept of a minimal state, denied its propensity towards interference in the market economy. Democracy, in this intellectual and ideological context, was conceived of in two ways, the one manifest in the rule of law and the institution of political elections, the other in the emergence (and strengthening) of a civil society, able to participate in the policy-making process and ensuring transparency and the accountability of publicly elected officials (Bhagwati, 1995; Dominguez and Lowenthal, 1996; Kaufmann, Kraay and Zoido-Lobatón, 1999).

At first the call and push for democracy in the direction of civil society — for democratizing the society-state relation — took the form of promoting nongovernmental organizations in the third sector, i.e., civil organizations without a profit orientation. Governmental and intergovernmental organizations such as the Organisation for Economic Co-operation and Development (OECD), the World Bank, etc. funded these organizations, converting them into their agents and leading to a proliferation of intermediary organizations vis-à-vis governments and international organizations on the one hand and local communities and grassroots organizations on the other. In the 1990s, however, there was a decided shift in the official discourse — and belatedly in the academic discourse — away from third-sector language towards a "strengthening of civil society" discourse. As Mitlin (1998) has determined, this shift reflected a shared interest of organizations involved in the development project in a more inclusive approach towards economic and social development — and thus supportive of a strategy, formulated in 1989 by the United Nations Development Programme (UNDP), designed to bring business associations and private capitalist enterprises into the development process at the level of poverty-reducing, employment-generating micro-projects and to foster the institution of good governance.

The Politics of Adjustment and Globalization:
Bad Government, Good Governance
Ethan Kapstein, Director of the U.S. Council of Foreign Relations (CFR) was one of the first to sound the alarm about the potentially destabilizing effects of globalization in its neoliberal form. As Kapstein (1996) saw it (also see Karl, 2000), excessive inequalities in income distribution and access to world society's productive resources resulting from economic globalization would generate politically destabilizing forces of social discontent and politi-

cal resistance, making it difficult for democratic regimes to stay the course of neoliberal policies and rendering the process as virtually ungovernable. Since Kapstein's warning, others — particularly, but by no means exclusively, economists at the World Bank — have echoed this concern, giving rise to a system-wide search for a new institutionality (architecture) that could establish good governance — order with as little "government" as possible (World Bank, 1994).

Good governance, in this context is predicated on a collaborative approach towards the politics of structural adjustment and globalization among the "stakeholders" in the process of economic and political development (Bardhan, 1997; Blair, 1997; UNDP, 1996; World Bank, 1994). What this means in practice is the engagement of civil society as a strategic partner in the process of securing the political conditions needed to implement an unpopular program of structural reforms (neoliberal policies). Second, it means a process of municipalization — shifting government administrative responsibilities from the central to local governments, converting municipalities into agents of economic and political development (BID 1996; Blair 1995, 1997; Mayorga 1997; Reilly 1989; Retolaza 2003; Sánchez 2003).

Third, it means the agency of nongovernmental organizations in turning the poor away from confrontational politics and the direct action of social movements towards alternative development — to seek improvements in their lives (micro-projects) within the local spaces available within the power structure, rather than challenging and seeking to change this structure. It means, in effect, reliance on a development strategy based on the accumulation of social capital, an approach that does not require substantive (i.e., structural) social change (radical reform or social transformation). This means the empowerment of the poor — making them feel engaged, positive about themselves and their situation, able to act on decisions that affect their lives and livelihoods (how to spend poverty-alleviation funds, identify and prioritize their needs and potential micro-projects, access micro-finance or set up micro-enterprises). It means imperialism in one of its diverse forms, on one of its many fronts.

Pax Americana: The Rise and Decline of the American Empire

> [Bush is] likely to learn the same lesson in the early 21st century that Theodore Roosevelt and Woodrow Wilson learned in the early 20th century.... When the United States goes out alone in search of monsters to destroy — venturing in terrain which imperial powers have already trod — it can itself become the monster. (John Judis, 2004)

17

The U.S. invasion of Afghanistan and the Iraq war have been presented as motivated by the geopolitical interest of the U.S. state in capturing a part of the world's major oil reserves. The Iraq war has also been understood by some (James Petras, for example) as a partial response to the power of the state of Israel and the U.S. Jewish lobby over U.S. Middle East policy. Undoubtedly both oil and Israel provide motives for the projection of U.S. military power in the Gulf region. However, an altogether more powerful explanation can be found in the concerns of a group of neoconservatives, which, under the presidency of George W. Bush, has captured the White House. Although these concerns relate directly to the perceived need to improve access to, if not more control over, the world's oil reserves, a greater concern of these neocons is to reassert U.S. hegemony over the world system — to re-establish the imperialist project of what Henry Luce, as early as 1941, termed the American Century. Paul Wolfowitz, one of these neocons, part of this White House gang and lead author of the notorious *Project for a New American Century*, proposed the unilateral projection of U.S. political and military power in the service of empire — to help the U.S. carry out its global responsibilities and its imperial burden, to free the world and secure the new American world order.[2]

In the immediate aftermath of the Second World War, the U.S. state had indeed achieved dominance and hegemony, accounting as it did for 38 percent of the world industrial production and 50 percent of the monetary gold and currency reserves. With just 6 percent of the world's population, the U.S. had over 59 percent of the world's developed oil reserves, generated 46 percent of electricity worldwide, and dominated world trade in goods and services.

With this power it had little difficulty in securing the stamp of U.S. foreign policy on the Bretton Woods world economic order. Notwithstanding its power, the existence of the U.S.S.R. and the socialist bloc and the challenge that they presented to the U.S. project of world dominance meant that the U.S. had to rely on multilateral action and a system of alliances, allies and satellite or client states. The parameters of this system were established at Bretton Woods and consolidated from the 1950s to the 1970s, not without the exercise of military power when and where it was needed to secure dominance and control. The U.S. state deemed Latin America to be well within its "sphere of influence" and its heads of state as satraps of the U.S. empire.

This entailed a series of invasions and other aggressive actions, some successful, others (Cuba) not. In the successful cases of Guatemala and the Dominican Republic, the invasions resulted in the ousting of less than fully compliant heads of state. In most of Latin America, however, imperial control was established primarily by means of a national security doctrine that entailed massive military aid in the form of training of Latin American armed forces, sponsorship and/or installation of military regimes, a counterinsurgency strategy directed against the guerrilla armies of national liberation and a "dirty war" of repression of "subversives," unionists, human rights and political activists, students and other domestic "enemies" waged by proxy (the U.S. military regimes installed by Washington). By these means, together with the Alliance for Progress — the soft glove and development arm of imperialism — the population in the region was more or less subjugated, and a complex of client states, beginning with Brazil in 1964 and Chile in 1973, was installed.

However, in the 1980s the empire began to fall apart as the U.S. experienced a series of losses around the world, except in its immediate backyard in Central America and in regions of lesser importance such as the Balkan states of Kosovo, Macedonia and Serbia. The loss of Vietnam was the catalyst for this decline in U.S. power, but in the 1980s the U.S. state experienced a series of additional defeats, losses and reversals, both in Asia and Europe and the Middle East/Gulf region. In Latin America, despite successes on some fronts, the U.S. failed to bring down the Castro regime in Cuba or defeat the FARC (Revolutionary Armed Forces of Columbia) in Colombia.

One reason why the erosion of U.S. military power brought about a conservative reaction to renovate the world order and restore the U.S. empire was that the a similar trend was occurring at the economic level. In the 1970s, the golden age of capitalism had come to an abrupt end and the world economy was in crisis. The U.S. had lost dominance, primarily *vis-à-vis* Japan and Germany but also Western Europe and a group of emerging "tigers" in Southeast Asia — the first of several tiers of NICs (newly industrialized countries) that proved to be formidable rivals of the U.S. in the battle for the world market. By the end of the decade, despite the U.S.'s unilateral move of abandoning the use of the gold standard to fix the international exchange rate, the U.S. had accumulated an enormous and growing balance-of-payment deficit, and its erstwhile dominant share of world trade continued to slide. In 1950, the U.S. accounted for 20 percent of world export trade, while Germany and Japan between them accounted for only 6.3 percent (Brenner 1998: 119). By 1970, the U.S. share had been cut 25 percent while Germany and Japan's combined share of world exports tripled to 18.8 percent. By 2000, notwithstanding the long boom of the 1990s, the U.S. share of world production and trade continued to slide relative to its competitors in both the E.U. and Asia, particularly China, whose annual output was growing at over 10 percent a year, almost triple the highest economic growth rate ever achieved by the U.S. economy.

In the 1980s, the U.S. response to the loss of economic and political dominance was threefold. First, the U.S. state redoubled its efforts regarding economic and other pressures on the U.S.S.R., which coincided with other largely internal pressures to bring about the collapse of the U.S.S.R. and the socialist bloc, allowing the U.S. to claim a victory in its war against international communism. Second, the U.S., through a complex of international financial institutions under its control, designed and installed a new world order and dictated the rules for client states to follow in adjusting their macroeconomic policies and opening up their economies to the forces of globalization by privatizing economic enterprise, deregulating markets and, above all, liberalizing trade and the flow of capital.

The result of this economic restructuring process is difficult to determine (the end is near but not here yet); it is a mixed bag at best, combining increased productivity of U.S. labour and profitability of U.S. capital, and a relatively sustained recovery of the U.S. economy, with growing resistance to the neoliberal globalization agenda not only from some recalcitrant states but from a global (and regionally located) civil society — powerful social movements that are challenging U.S. power. In Latin America, these forces of resistance have spawned powerful anti-globalization, anti-imperialist movements, which have derailed the U.S. agenda of a regional free market and spawned a new wave of left-of-centre regimes disposed to bring about another world, if not an alternative system.

The U.S.'s third response to multiple continuing crises was to launch, under the presidency of George W. Bush and the neocon ascendancy over U.S. foreign policy, another counteroffensive, redoubling its efforts thereby to restore U.S. dominance and hegemony. This imperial counteroffensive took diverse forms: (1) policies and efforts, including the invasion of Afghanistan and Iraq, designed to re-establish the subordination of Europe to Washington; (2) reassertion of control in the Middle East and Gulf region; (3) deepening and extending military penetration in Latin America and Asia; (4) increased pressures on and military warfare against FARC in Colombia; (5) the projection of economic and military power in the rest of the continent; (6) the incorporation of the private sector into the development process and a concerted effort to launch the war on global poverty with the assistance of strategic partners including NGOs and local governments; (7) efforts to repress protest and opposition against the multinational corporations and international financial institutions (IFIs) like the World Bank, the International Monetary Fund and World Trade Organization (replacing democratic rights with dictatorial powers); and (8) the use of state spending on weapons and subsidies for near bankrupt U.S. multinationals (airlines, insurance companies, tourist agencies) and regressive tax reductions to halt a deepening recession, which would undermine public support for the empire-building project, particularly in the context of growing military expenditures on the war on terrorism.

Notwithstanding the onslaught of counteroffensive actions and the projection of economic and military power, the U.S. has not managed to secure and consolidate its empire. In Latin America, the new millennium has seen a tilt towards the left and the emergence of a distinct anti-U.S. (i.e., anti-imperialist, anti-globalization) state alliance. At the level of trade and investment, Latin America is seeking to diversify relations, turning in particular to China, which Hugo Chavez has noted, is a world power but does not come to Latin America with "imperialist airs." More important, Chinese investors are willing to accept lower profit margins than their U.S. or European competitors, strengthening the hands of governments seeking to tighten the terms of concessions in oil, gas and other sectors. For Brazil and Argentina, the two biggest economies in the region, China is also seen as a political counterweight to U.S. imperialism and an ally in the WTO (World Trade Organisation) and other arenas. Elsewhere in the world, the empire has proven to be equally fragile, infested with conflict and surrounded by growing forces of opposition and resistance. China and India have entered into an alliance of sorts with Russia in regard to the "big game" of Eurasia's massive reserves of natural resources. U.S. geopolitical strategy in this regard — seeking to divide Russia from its erstwhile satellite states and gain access to the region's oil, gas and other resources — is not bearing fruit; nor is its costly venture into Iraq or posturing regarding Iran. Despite the massive mobilization of financial and military resources, the U.S. empire in every area of strategic geopolitical interest is under siege.

Conclusion

The dynamics of social change analyzed in this book can only be understood in the context of conditions generated by the workings of three macroeconomic strategic projects and associated worldwide events. The first of these was international development, a project designed in 1948 as a means of thwarting pressures on the newly independent states in the "economically backward" areas of the world from the U.S.S.R. and the Soviet bloc of countries to take a socialist path towards nation-building and national reconstruction. The ideology of developmentalism served the U.S. for three decades as a model for state-led development and as a means of offsetting and averting pressures for more radical change. The second was globalization, a doctrine invented in the 1980s as a means of re-establishing U.S. ideological and economic hegemony over the world system. Globalization has been presented as a form of development, the best if not only way of bringing about economic growth and placing countries on the road towards a future of prosperity. But the projects of international cooperation for both development and globalization can be seen as masks for an entirely different project — U.S. imperialism. Notwithstanding recent efforts to move beyond the Washington Consensus, the ideology of globalization continues to serve as the basic template of the structural reforms that every state is expected to implement as a condition for entry into the club of industrialized rich countries.

The third project, U.S. imperialism, has been implemented in diverse forms, old and new, ranging from local development to war. It is responsible, more or less, for the relative failure of governments and people in Latin America to make substantial gains over the years in improving the living and working conditions of the population, 40 to 60 percent of which (80 percent in some rural contexts) is mired in poverty. This population, however, is not quietly lying down, accepting its fate and bearing the brunt of U.S. policy. A burgeoning civil society in the region, at least in its popular sector, is emerging, strengthened it seems somewhat ironically by the very moves of U.S. imperialism to defend itself from its enemies within.

Notes

1. In academic and political circles there is much talk and writing today about the "new imperialism," with reference to a project of empire building constructed by a group of neocons that have surrounded and entered the administration of George W. Bush. The literature on this is becoming voluminous. However, there is considerable evidence that this project, even in its projection of naked military power and resort to unilateral action and preemptive strikes, is not at all "new" — that it can be traced out in virtually every administration in the twentieth century, both Republican and Democratic, liberal and conservative, and not least in Clinton's administration (Leffler, 2004).

2. The document *Project for a New American Century* was drafted eight years after the Wolfowitz Report. It draws much of its inspiration and its policy recommendations from this report and like it is saturated with the belief in the moral and military supremacy of the U.S.

Chapter 2

Banking on Poverty

Economists have long argued that growth is based on a capital accumulation process, advanced via an increase in the rate of national savings and investment. The theory, articulated by, among others, Sir Arthur Lewis, a pioneer of development economics from the Caribbean, has been widely used to justify a policy of reducing the share of labour (wages) in national income. The idea is that workers and households have a low capacity to save and invest and that they tend to spend all or most of their income. This spending keeps up demand for goods and services, and thus expands the domestic market, but it does nothing to generate economic growth. The rich generally, and capitalists more particularly, have a higher propensity to save and invest. Thus, if the income available to this class increases, via wage compression and a reduction in the share of labour in national income (via the reversion of progressive taxation and income redistribution social programs), then economic growth will result.

This thinking, put into practice in the 1970s and 1980s as part of a protracted class war between labour and capital, resulted in a reduction in the share of labour (and households) in national incomes and thus an increase in the inequitable distribution of this income as well as the growth of poverty in the midst of wealth. The impact of this pro-capital (pro-growth) policy on the social distribution of national incomes is discussed below, but the most dramatic effect of the policy was wage compression, with wages in many cases (the U.S., for example) losing at least 10 percent of their average value from 1974 to 1984 and anywhere from 5 to 40 percent in the following decades (even more in some of the developing countries in Sub-Saharan Africa and Latin America). In many Latin American countries, such as Argentina, average per capita income in 2000 was less than it was in 1970. And the share of labour in national income in many cases was reduced by as much and more than 50 percent in the process — from around 40 percent in the not atypical cases of Chile and Mexico to below 20 percent. In East Asia — in South Korea, for example, or China in recent years — this trend is even more accentuated, with governments pursuing policies that result in a national savings and investment rate of over 30 and in some cases (Singapore, China) 40 percent. What this means is that workers in these countries work long hours for low wages, very low in the case of China, thus making a "contribution to national development" (rapid economic growth). It also means that the capitalist class has appropriated virtually all of the new wealth generated over the course of this period, a well-documented fact in the case of the U.S.[1]

The capitalist class in these countries, whether or not it invested productively its share of national income, not only was in the driver's seat of the growth engine but has profited immensely. In Mexico, for example, one individual, Carlos Slim, a multibillionaire and the richest man by far in Latin America (third on *Forbes'* list of the world's richest), after twelve years of market-friendly neoliberal policies in Mexico, including the privatization of Telmex, has ended up with a personal fortune greater than the combined income of all the country's indigenous peoples, some 14 percent of a population of 80 million. In one year alone (2003) it was reported that his personal income grew by 88 percent. And Slim is by no means alone in this. For Latin America, *Forbes's* list includes thirty-three "men of business" who share a collective fortune of USD114 billion, double the total of FDI inflows in 2005 and equivalent to the annual combined income of the region's poor, 160 million forced to subsist on less than USD$2 a day.

The Failure of Neoliberals to Promote Economic Growth

The new economic model of structural reform was widely implanted in the 1980s and the 1990s with the promise of a new dawn — entry into the road to prosperity paved by foreign investment attracted by a market friendly approach towards national development. By the end of the 1990s, however, after three rounds and two decades of experiments with neoliberal policy reforms, the Promised Land was receding into the horizon. First, neoliberalism failed utterly to deliver on the promised economic growth. Harvard University economist Dani Rodrik (1997), no radical political economist, cites dismal growth performance during the 1990s as the most damaging evidence of the failure of neoliberalism. The facts are clear: two decades of neoliberalism failed to generate economic growth. Worldwide, an annually averaged per capita growth rate over the preceding period of state-led development and interventionism was reduced by half, from 3 to 1.5 percent in the industrialized countries; in the developing countries (excluding China and India), the average rate of growth was reduced from an average of around 3.5 percent in the era of government intervention to 1.2 percent during the neoliberal era (1980–2000); as for the poorest countries, the rate of growth over the same period was reduced from a modest 1.9 percent increase in GDP (gross domestic product) to a decline of 0.5 percent per year (Chang and Grabel, 2004: 17).

Countries at every level of per capita GDP performed worse during the neoliberal era than in the two preceding decades. The only exceptions to this trend were in a group of Asian newly industrializing countries (the World Bank's "eight rapidly growing countries," notably China but also

India), whose governments continued to pursue an essentially interventionist approach, eschewing neoliberal policies in their path towards national development. Some economists have argued the existence of a trend towards convergence in the growth rates of developed and developing countries. However, this trend is accounted for entirely by the acceleration of growth in the two largest developing countries, namely China and India — countries that in no sense followed the neoliberal policy formula. As for Latin America, per capita GDP for the entire region grew by 75 percent from 1960 to 1980 but only 7 percent in the subsequent neoliberal era, 1980–2000 (ibid: 17). And the situation in Sub-Saharan Africa, where governments everywhere turned towards neoliberalism in the 1980s, an accumulated growth rate of 34 percent turned into a decline of 15 percent over the same period.

That neoliberalism has not delivered on its promise of economic growth is just the beginning of the problem. Even worse is the fact that the anaemic growth achievements of its policy regime have been accompanied by numerous and onerous adverse consequences in other areas, particularly in regards to disparities in access to productive resources and the distribution of wealth and income. In this area neoliberalism has been indicted by a broad array of analysts, including erstwhile advocates. The dimensions of this problem can be analyzed at various levels — along the North-South global divide, among countries across the world system and within countries both North and South.

The Inequality Predicament

When China and India are not factored into the analysis, available data show a rise in worldwide income inequality, owing to the combined effect of higher income disparities within countries and the adverse distributive effect of faster population growth in poorer countries. As shown in Table 2.1, the income gap between the richest and poorest countries has widened over the course of the neoliberal era of globalizing capital and neoimperialism. The table shows inequalities in the distribution of income among world regions, presenting the per capita income in each region as a percentage of per capita income in the rich OECD (industrialized) countries as a group, as well as the changes in these ratios over the past two decades. The data in these and other studies (see, in particular Pochmann et al., 2004) reveal a trend towards increasing international disparities in income distribution and a connection between this trend and the turn towards neoliberal policies. In the *Atlas of Social Exclusion* (2004), constructed by Pochmann and colleagues over the past two decades, twenty-eight countries improved their standing on an index of social inequalities and exclusion; these countries, all found in the developed centre of the global economy, represent 14.4 percent of world population but account for 52.1 percent of world annual income (and, of course, a much

Table 2.1 Per Capita Income as a Percentage of OECD,
by Developing Region (per capita, in constant USD)

	1980	1981–85	1986–90	1991–95	1996–00	2001
Sub-Saharan Africa	3.3	3.1	2.5	2.1	2.0	1.9
Latin America/ Caribbean	18.0	16.0	14.2	13.5	13.3	12.8
South Asia	1.2	1.3	1.3	1.4	1.5	1.6
East Asia	1.5	1.7	1.9	2.5	3.1	3.3

Source: UNESCO, 2005: 46.

larger percentage of wealth, most of which is neither earned nor measured in available statistics). Sixty countries, representing 35.5 percent of world population, account for only 11.1 percent of world income. Of the countries with the highest indices of poverty, social exclusion and income inequality, forty-one are in Africa; ten are in Asia; and six are in the Americas.

The figures in Table 2.1 indicate that per capita income in all developing regions, except South Asia, East Asia and the Pacific, has declined relative to the high-income OECD countries. Per capita income levels in Sub-Saharan Africa, the Middle East and North Africa, and Latin America and the Caribbean have been steadily declining relative to the average per capita income in the wealthier OECD countries. Between 1980 and 2001 these levels decreased from 3.3 to 1.9 percent in Sub-Saharan Africa, from 9.7 to 6.7 percent in the Middle East and North Africa, and from 18 to 12.8 percent in Latin America and Caribbean. The change in these ratios indicates not that per capita income in developing regions has decreased in absolute terms but that per capita income has grown faster in the richer regions than in the poorer ones, widening the inequality gap.

Table 2.2 points to a general trend towards increasing divergence under the new economic model and away from the convergence predicted by the advocates of free market policies. Neoliberalism has induced a rising inequality among countries, particularly along the North-South divide, partly as a result of a concentration of private capital flows and partly as a result of conditions generated by policies of structural adjustment designed as a means of attracting foreign investment.

Notwithstanding the economic growth of recent years and evidence of a recovery from the production crisis of the early 1970s, what best defines neoliberalism in practice is a pattern of uneven development and the growth

Table 2.2 Widening Regional Income Gap (GDP per capita)
(1985 PPP US$)

	1960	Dif. from OECD	2000	Dif. from OECD
OECD	6,200	-	17,000	-
Latin America	2,000	4,200	4,900	12,100
East Asia	500	5,700	2,500	14,500
South Asia	800	5,400	1,400	15,600
Sub-Saharan Africa	750	5,450	700	16,300

Source: UNDP 2001, 2004.

of social inequalities in the distribution of income. The UNDP finds that in 1960 the countries with the richest quintile of the world's population had aggregate income thirty times that of those countries with the poorest 20 percent. By 1980, at the outset of the neoliberal era, the ratio had risen to 45 to 1; by 1989, it stood at 59 to 1; and by 1997, a full decade and a half into the neoliberal experience, it had risen to a staggering 70 to 1 (UNDP, 1996, 1999, 2001). The situation of people in the poorest countries worsened relative to those in the middle-income and higher income group. In 1960, for example, per capita income in Sub-Saharan Africa was about 11 percent of per capita income in the industrialized countries. By 1998 it was only 4 percent and in 2003 it was barely 3 percent.

Over the course of the neoliberal policy period the income disparity between the richest and poorest countries nearly doubled, reviving an earlier debate about the connection between economic growth and social inequality. This issue was at the centre of a theoretical and policy debate in the 1970s, but in this new context the debate was re-opened and is ongoing, mostly involving economists at or associated with the World Bank (Banerjee and Duflo, 2003; Deininger and Squire, 1998; Dollar and Kraay, 2002; Forbes, 2000; Klasen, 2005; Ravallion, 2004).

As in bygone years, the key issue in this debate is whether social inequality inhibits or promotes economic growth. However, the focus in this new context of globalization (i.e., imperialism) was on unequal access to society's productive resources and wealth rather than income distribution. And it was more or less understood that a minimal degree of greater equality in this regard was a precondition for growth and that excessive inequality inhibits growth, because of its exclusion of a large number of individuals who are potentially productive. As for the policy of government interference in the redistribution of market-generated incomes, the issue was viewed differently. At this level, the old dogma was trotted out to the effect that an unequal distribution of income — or, what amounts to the same, increased participation of capital in national income, the acknowledged outcome of free market policies — is a good policy: it functions as a motivating device, providing an incentive to produce, a catalyst of economic growth. This is the theory; the facts are quite otherwise. At issue here is the presumption of a built-in tendency towards a convergence of income levels after an initial income gap, which is needed as an incentive to capitalist entrepreneurs, who have a higher propensity to invest than workers. The theory is that allowing market forces to operate freely without government interference will eventually allow the poor to participate in the fruits of economic growth. Once the seeds of economic growth have been sown, a part of the enlarged national income will trickle down to the poor, resulting in a sort of inverted income curve. With reference to this theory, which was initially advanced in the 1950s by Kuznets, World Bank economists have begun to write of their "pro-growth" policies as "pro-poor" (Kakwani and Pernia (2000).

The magnitude of the global income divide and associated problems is staggering. The richest quintile of the world's people consume 86 percent of all products — everything from meat to paper and automobiles — while the poorest quintile consumes only 1.3 percent. The OECD, with 19 percent of the world's population, in 1998 accounted for 80 percent of the world's GNP (Gross National Product), 71 percent of world trade and 58 percent of foreign investment (UNDP, 1999: 3). And more recent data suggest that little has changed, except for the relative advance of China and India, admittedly a large part of the total picture, so much so that inclusion of these two populous countries hides the growing development gap in the rest of the world. Within the structure of this gap, the three richest persons in the world have assets that exceed the combined GDP of the 48 poorest countries. In fact, if the poorest 47 percent of the world (about 2.7 billion persons) were to pool their incomes they could barely purchase the assets of the world's wealthiest 225 individuals, the super-rich (UNDP, 1999: 3). These individuals, representing 1 percent of the richest 1 percent in the world, control a staggering 24 percent of global wealth (Kundnani, 2006: 27). A tax of 4 percent on this wealth, or a one percent tax on the speculative unproductive transactions in the world's capital markets, would be more than enough to pay for basic and adequate health care, food, clean water and safe sewers for every person on earth.

Apart from the question of meeting the basic needs of the world's population — of lifting over 2.6 billion people, mostly in the developing countries, out of their poverty — these social inequalities, particularly in regard to the conditions of absolute poverty (associated, by the World Bank, with income of under $1 a day), which affect at least 1.5 billion, have severe damaging effects, including malnutrition and diseases that reduce both the quality and the length of life. It is estimated that up to 150 million children a year — 4,500 a day from poor sanitation alone — die from these effects, conditions that are structurally determined and quite remediable considering the idea of taxing the inordinate wealth of the rich.

Mark Weisbrot, Dean Baker, Egor Kraev and Judy Chen (2001) at the Center for Economic and Policy Research (CEPR) put the neoliberal hypothesis — that if the poor countries were to let their economies be dominated by private capital and the free market, they would converge with the rich countries — to the test. They divided countries into five groups, from the poorest to the richest. Then they compared how these countries fared between 1960 and 1980 (before the introduction of neoliberal policies) and from 1980 to 2000 (when these policies were widely embraced). Their results are revealing of the impact of neoliberal policies, touted by the World Bank as "pro-poor" (World Bank 2004a), on economic growth and social inequality. They found that the performance of the poorest countries got considerably worse relative to the rich countries, that is, there was no convergence either in regard to wealth or income. On the contrary, the rich got richer and the poor became poorer, a pattern that holds up for national distributions of income as well. Overall, social inequalities in the distribution of wealth and income, both within and among countries, and the social divide between the North and South increased over the period of neoliberal structural reform.

Nevertheless, the issue has not been settled by the revelations of these facts and the arguments presented by the UNDP (1999) in regard to the transition countries and Asia, and by the Economic Commission for Latin America and the Caribbean (ECLAC 2002) in regard to Latin America. The economists at the World Bank and the IMF continue to argue the need for neoliberal structural reforms, against all the evidence and arguments advanced by revisionists such as Joseph Stiglitz and Dani Rodrik. The argument is that governments should stay the course and extend these reforms. The medicine prescribed by the IMF and World Bank as far back as 1983, it is argued, is the best way to bring about prosperity for all and ultimately benefit the poor. The claim is that the failure in economic performance of so many developing countries and the lack of a global income convergence can be attributed to the failure of governments to fully implement the recommended reforms.

Disparities Within: The Predicament in Its Local Dimension

The neoliberal counter-revolution has deepened the global income and wealth divide, but, as shown in the U.N.'s most recent social development report, *The Inequality Predicament* (UNESCO, 2005), it has also deepened inequalities within countries, both North and South. In addition, the report shows that income inequality has grown faster in countries such as the U.S. and the U.K., which have thoroughly embraced the neoliberal doctrine, than in countries that have not (UNESCO, 2005: 18). In these countries, particularly the U.S., analysts have documented the growing gap between the very rich and the very poor and a rapidly shrinking middle class (Chang and Grabel, 2004; 21).

This pattern of a growing income gap within countries both North and South, and the connection between this pattern and the turn towards neoliberalism, also shows up in other studies. For example, data provided by the World Income Inequality Database (WIID) shows that within-country income inequality decreased during the 1950s, 1960s and 1970s in most developed, developing and centrally planned economies, but that since the 1980s this decline has slowed or levelled off, and that within many countries income inequality is on the rise, in some cases dramatically so. Under the conditions of this rise in income inequality and as the direct result of the dismantling of the socialist state, Cornia, Addison and Kiiski (2004) discovered that in the countries that once constituted the socialist bloc, income inequality from 1989 to 1996 rose by an average of 10 to 20 Gini points and the number of people living in poverty jumped from 14 million in 1989 to 147 million (see also Table 2.4).

The Gini index of income inequality is the most commonly used summary measure of national income distribution. The Gini index for most countries has increased over the past two decades of neoliberalism and imperialism. In the U.S., for example, it is 17 percent higher than in 1980. In Latin America, the region showing the greatest disparities in national income distribution, income disparities have increased dramatically over the past two and a half decades. In the 1950s, 1960s and into the 1970s, the structured inequalities in income distribution were on the decline, the result of an economic model and developmental states that slowly incorporated workers, producers and the middle class into the economic development process, providing improvements in their access to society's productive resources and to government social and development programs. With a conservative (neoliberal) counter-revolution and sweeping reforms in national policy that restructured the economies in the region and facilitated their integration into the world economy, this process was halted and reversed in the 1980s. The outcome, marked by a process of privatization, financial liberalization, market deregulation and downsizing, was visible some years later in an extension of structured inequalities in income distribution, with a consequent deepening of the conditions of poverty and wealth at the extremes of this distribution.

Over the course of the 1980s and 1990s, the share of labour (wages and salaries) in national income was reduced in many cases by half — from 40 percent plus in Chile, for example, to below 20 percent. A clear reflection of these developments and their outcomes is in the ratio of incomes received by the poorest quintile of households, a useful and revealing unit of analysis, to those received by the richest 20 percent. In most countries this ratio was comparatively high to begin with — 18 to 1 in the case of Brazil — but it increased in every case except perhaps Chile.

According to ECLAC (2002: 83), at the turn towards the new millennium, 83.8 percent of the population in Latin America live in countries with worsening inequality. As for Chile, the government's apparent success in avoiding the economic contraction and increased social inequalities that accompanied the structural adjustment process in other countries is the direct result of its imposition, in 1998, of a regime of "capital control" — a reserve requirement tax of 30 percent on FDI, a one-year residence requirement on both PI (portfolio investment) and FDI, and a severe restriction on the freedom of pension fund managers to invest their assets abroad (Chang and Grabel, 2004: 132).[2] As a result of its restrictive approach to foreign investment and an expansion of its social investment policy, Chile began to experience a significant reduction in private capital inflows in August 1998. The upside of this trend was macroeconomic stability and an improvement in the distribution of national income. Chile and Colombia (which also imposed capital controls) were the only major countries in the region able to escape the devastating after-effects of the Mexican and Asian financial crises.

Recent studies show a persistent pattern of growing social inequalities associated with structural reform in macroeconomic policy. In the case of Mexico, a study by the Instituto Nacional de Estadística, Geografía e Informática (INEGI, 2004) showed that from 2000 to 2004 the only part of the population that increased its share of national income was the richest quintile of households (*La Jornada*, June 14, 2005). The bottom quintile's share of national income remains unchanged at 1.6 percent. This 1.6 percent corresponds to the income share of the poorest fifth of Latin America's population. Some 220 million, 44 percent of the region's total population are classified by the World Bank as poor (earning less than $2 per day) while 96 million are extremely poor (earning less than $1 a day); as for the richest quintile, their average share of total regional income is 48 percent, while in Mexico, according to INEGI, it is 52.7 percent, up 1.3 percentage points in just two years of a deepening of neoliberal policies under the presidency of Vicente Fox. Thirty-nine percent of the extremely poor, those who have to survive with less than a dollar a day, are found in Mexico and Brazil, both regional champions of neoliberalism.

The statistics are an eloquent testimony to neoliberalism's social legacy: to build the prosperity of the few — such as Mexico's eleven billionaires, whose combined income exceeds that of the country's 40 million poor — on the exploitation, degradation and misery of the many, on low wages and shattered dreams. ~~It is about foreign investment, which works like a suction pump, leading to a massive unregulated outflow of financial and productive resources, both financial and human and~~, as a result, banking, currency and financial crises and an increase in inequality, poverty and immiseration. It is about "~~freedom~~," the banner of which is waved about so much by the ideologues of neoliberalism. But how many of the world's poor — over 2.5 billion who cannot meet their basic needs — are free to choose, free to make decisions that might improve the quality of their lives, free from exploitation and oppression, free from the operations of capital freed from all constraints and "interference"?

The Inequality Predicament in Argentina

A 2006 report titled *La dueda interna se acentua: Ingresos, salarios y convenios colectivos en Argentina 2006*, by a commission headed by Claudio Lozana, Congressional Deputy in Argentina's parliament, provides a close look at what the United Nations has described as "the inequality predicament." The report also proves a revealing window on this chapter's topic: FDI in its social dimension. What the congressional commission discovered was that the recent post-crisis spurt of economic growth, averaging over 7 percent a year since 2003, is associated with a notable increase of social inequality in the distribution of incomes generated in this period.

After years into one of the worst economic crises of the twentieth century, Argentina has experienced the highest rate of economic growth in the entire region. By several accounts this growth was stimulated by government policy, particularly the decision to suspend payments on the foreign debt and to productively invest the resulting savings, and by an economic reactivation process led by the investments of the largest corporations, many of which are foreign-owned. However, what Lozano and his team found was that the contribution of labour to productivity growth was not duly remunerated — far from it.

While in the largest 1000 corporations, the contribution of labour to annual production was valued at around $120,000 per worker, the average wage received by the workers at the end of 2005 was only $722, an exceedingly and excessively high rate of exploitation that, the report concluded, represented only 32.7 percent of the cost of the basket of goods and services needed by households to cover the essentials of life (*canasta básica*). And the situation was even worse for the 100 largest corporations, about half of which are foreign-owned. Each worker added $200,000 to the value of production but was remunerated on average with a wage of $2379. The report concludes that, given the productivity of labour, wages could easily be increased fourfold and need to be increased minimally by 45 percent — to the level of the *canasta básica*.

Lozana and his team drew a number of conclusions that have a direct bearing on the relation of FDI (reflected in the operations of the largest corporations) to economic growth and its impact on the distribution of household income. The report notes, assuming two workers per household earning on average $722 each and receiving an additional $60 in the form of family welfare, average household income at the end of 2005 was $1,564, 30 percent less than the cost of basic goods and services. For those working in the informal sector, an estimated 43 percent of the labour force, average income ($632) is below the household poverty line ($860), and for households composed of informal sector workers, average income represents only 57.3 percent of the *canasta básica*. Thus, even households composed of two income earners, difficult enough in a situation of high unemployment, are unable to rise out of poverty. As a result, the poor today encompasses close to half of households and an even higher percentage of the total population, reaching well into what used to be one of the strongest middle classes in Latin America. By official government estimates, one half of this class today is now poor and constitutes a large part of the "new poor."

The Lozano Report clearly connects this inequality predicament not only to government policy but to the operations of capital in the free market and the capital-labour relation. The authors show that while productivity in the industrial sector from 2001 to 2005 grew by 12.4 percent (representing a reduction of 35.9 percent in labour costs) real wages grew only 0.4 percent. This deterioration in the capital-labour relation and in the share of labour in national income and value added, is clearly reflected in the abysmally low level of average wages, which at the end of 2005 barely reached a level achieved in 1970. Total wages represent only 25.6 percent of value added to production by the 1000 largest companies, and only 19.9 percent of value added for the 100 largest (Table 2.3).

José Blanco, a columnist for *La Jornada*, notes, with reference to Mexico, where income distribution is similar to Argentina's, that "inequality is not poverty" (25 April, 2006). The point he makes is that the increased disparities in income distribution found across Latin America, and which are clearly the result of government policies of financial and trade liberalization and privatization of assets and enterprises, does not necessarily translate into more poverty. And indeed several studies by the Comisión Económica para América Latina (CEPAL) and the World Bank seem to bear this out. Despite the stark inequality predicament documented for Argentina — and notwithstanding the fact that household incomes and wages in a context of rapid economic growth keep many working-class households immersed in poverty — these studies have determined that the poverty rate in recent years has declined somewhat both in Argentina and elsewhere in the region, even in countries such as Mexico and Peru, where social inequalities have worsened.

Table 2.3 Economic Variables, 1000 and 100 Largest Corporations, Argentina 2003

	1,000 top	100 top
Gross value added, in pesos millions	73,496	47,592
Wages (V), in pesos millions	18,839	8,503
Surplus value (S)	54,657	39,089
Wages (V)/Gross value added	25.6%	17.9%
Number of wage workers	609,243	245,019
Value added/workers (pesos per month)	120,635	194,239
Av. wages (pesos per month)	2,379	2,669
Productivity per worker (pesos per month)	9,290	14,941
Surplus value per corp. (pesos per month)	4,564,750	32,574,417
Surplus value per month/wage	1,915	12,203

Source: Lozana, 2006; elaborated on the basis of INDEC, *Censo Nacional Económico de 2004.*

Presumably this amelioration in the number of people in dire straits, i.e., those earning less than $1 a day (the World Bank's standard of extreme poverty), is the result of corrective action taken by governments and intergovernmental organizations in their "war against poverty." But as we see below the issue is by no means so simple.

Living the Washington Consensus: The Social Face of Neoliberalism

From Stagnation to Class Crisis

To sustain their profits under conditions of chronic stagnation, the Latin American capitalist class has periodically engaged in direct assaults on the working class, attacking its organizational and negotiating capacity. It has also engaged in an indirect assault (via the state) on social benefits, reversing the social legislation of the previous period to undermine the capacity of labour to participate in productivity gains. Very little of the capital attracted to the region has been invested productively. Over the course of the 1980s and 1990s, the rate of participation of capital in productivity gains has been negative or marginal. Labour has participated substantially in productivity growth, but it has done so without a corresponding increase in its level of share of productivity gains. In fact, the share of labour in the value added to production and national income (Table 2.4) has been drastically reduced by labour restructuring. Thus the working class has undoubtedly borne the

Table 2.4 Wages as a Percentage of National Income

	1970	1980	1985	1989	1992
Argentina	40.9	31.5	31. 2	-	24.9
Chile	47.7	43.4	27.8	19.0	-
Ecuador	34.4	34.8	23.6	16.0	15.8
Mexico	37.5	39.0	31.6	28.4	27.3
Peru	40.0	32.8	30.5	25.5	16.8

Source: CEPAL, several years.

brunt of the structural adjustment generated by efforts to insert the Latin American economy into the globalization process.

The source of this "structural adjustment" is the restructuring of labour in its forms of employment (creating more precariousness), its conditions of work (causing more irregularity and informality) and in its relation to capital. The process can be seen at two levels. It is reflected first of all in conditions that have resulted in a significant reduction of the share of labour in national incomes (and value added). For example, under the Allende regime, Chilean labour received well over half of the national income. By 1980, however, after five years of crisis and draconian anti-labour measures, this share was reduced to 43 percent, and by 1989, after seventeen years of military dictatorship and free market reforms, to 19 percent. In other countries can be found variations on the same theme. On average, the share of labour (wages) in national income has been reduced from around 40 percent at the beginning of the adjustment process to less than 20 percent, and this development has been paralleled by an even greater reduction in the share of labour in the value added to the social product. Other structural changes can be seen in the reduction of jobs in the formal sector of production and in an associated decline and disappearance of the industrial proletariat.

Structural change in the working class, particularly in regard to the growth of the informal sector of street work, has also been evident in the fall in the value of wages and the worsening of wide disparities in the distribution of earned incomes among households. In many cases, wage levels in the early 1990s were still well below levels of previous periods. The Bank of Mexico estimates that at the end of 1994, that is, before the later outbreak of crisis, wages had maintained barely 40 percent of their 1980 value. In Venezuela and Argentina workers have not yet recovered wage levels achieved in 1970.

As for unequal distribution of income and compression of wages, Argentina provides the exemplar: in 1975 the ratio of income received by the top and bottom quintiles of income earners was 8 to 1, but by 1991 this gap had doubled, and by 1997 it was a staggering 25 to 1. In the extreme but not atypical case of Brazil, the top 10 percent of income earners receive forty-four times more income than the bottom. And in other countries we witness the same growing social inequalities in the distribution of wealth and income — at one extreme, the sprouting of a handful of huge fortunes and an associated process of capital accumulation and, at the other, the spread and deepening of grinding poverty. ECLAC estimates that over the period of structural reforms implemented in the 1980s, the rate of poverty in the region increased from 35 percent to 41 percent of the population (or, using the World Bank's more conservative and very problematic measure of $2 a day, from 27 to 28 percent). But according to ECLAC, from 1993 to 1996, the incidence and rate of poverty was reduced in eight of the twelve countries it examined, a trend reversed later in the decade when an emerging pattern of low growth led ECLAC to see the beginnings of another decade lost to development. A closer look at the statistics provided by the World Bank, and used by ECLAC, suggests that the observed reduction in the rate of poverty (see Table 2.5) involved either sleight of hand or outright obfuscation and lies: the rate of poverty was reduced by redefining the poverty line according to the World Bank's base measure of $2 a day ($1 for the rate of absolute poverty or indigence). By the earlier, more reasonable measure, related to the capacity of the population to meet its basic needs, the rate of poverty has continued to climb — up to a half of all households by some estimates, at least 40 percent according to the latest ECLAC study (2005). In any case, the minimal progress identified for Latin America in the mid-1990s disappeared soon thereafter. In Sub-Saharan Africa, North Africa and the Middle East, South Asia and the countries "in transition," even when using the World Bank's conservative measure of poverty, the number of the poor increased by 195 million from 1993 to 2001. In the countries in transition from socialism to capitalism (East Europe/Central Asia), the number of the poor increased dramatically in the immediate aftermath of the collapse of the socialist regime, not the result of statistical fiat but of an abrupt change in government policy. In just three years, from 1990 to 1993, the percentage of the poor jumped from 5 to 17 percent.

The adjustment of workers to the demands of imperialism is reflected politically in the destruction of their class organizations and in a generalized weakening of their capacity to negotiate collective agreements with capital. These developments, as well as the notable failure or incapacity everywhere of the working class to resist the imperial imposition of the neoliberal agenda, reflect a new correlation of class forces. In the 1970s, workers confronted a concentration of armed force and repression, as well as a direct assault by capital on their organizational capacities and conditions of social existence.

Table 2.5 Poverty Rates for the World, Major Regions, and India and China

	1981	1984	1987	1990	1993	1996	1999	2001
Number of people living on less than USD2 per day (millions)								
Sub-Sahara Africa	288	326	355	382	410	447	489	516
Middle East/Nth Africa	52	50	53	51	52	61	70	70
Latin America/ Caribbean	99	119	115	125	136	117	127	128
Europe/Central Asia	20	18	15	23	81	98	113	93
South Asia	821	859	911	958	1005	1029	1039	1064
East Asia	1170	1109	1028	1116	1079	922	900	864
China	876	814	731	825	803	650	627	594
India	630	662	697	731	770	807	805	826
World	2450	2480	2478	2654	2764	2674	2739	2735
Percentage of people living on less than USD2 per day								
Sub-Sahara Africa	73	76	76	75	75	75	75	76
Middle East/Nth Africa	29	25	24	21	20	22	24	23
Latin America/ Caribbean	27	30	28	28	30	24	25	25
Europe/Central Asia	5	4	3	5	17	21	24	20
South Asia	89	87	87	86	85	82	78	77
East Asia	85	77	68	70	65	53	50	47
China	88	79	67	73	68	53	50	47
India	90	88	87	86	86	85	81	80

Source: UNESCO, 2005: 52–53.

In the 1980s the major mechanism of adjustment was the restructuring of the capital-labour relation based on forces released during the change in economic policy.

In the 1990s, within the same institutional and policy framework, the working class also confronted a major campaign by organizations such as the World Bank for labour market reform. The aim of this campaign was to create political conditions for a new and more flexible regime of capital accumulation and mode of labour regulation: to give capital, in its management function, more freedom to hire, fire and use labour as needed; and to render labour more flexible, that is, disposed to accept wages offered under free market conditions and to submit to the new management model of its relation to capital and the organization of production. As the World Bank sees it, widespread government interference in the labour market and workplace (e.g., minimum wage legislation), as well as excessive (monopoly) union power, have distorted the workings of the market, leading capital to withdraw from the production process and thereby generating the problems of unemployment, poverty and informality that plague the region.

To resolve these "problems," labour legislation protecting employment have been replaced by laws that enhance the arbitrary power of employers to fire workers, reduce compensation for firings and hire temporary and casual labour. Such deregulation of labour and other markets has led to new rules that facilitate new investments and the transfer of profits, but also result in massive decimation of stable jobs for workers, increased marginality for and within many communities, and sharply polarized national economies.

Disparities in income distribution and access to productive resources are reflected, at one extreme, in a concentration of income within the capitalist class and the spawning of a number of huge fortunes. Worse, much of the income available to this class is undeclared. For example, revenues from narcotrafficking by capitalists in Mexico, the proceeds of which are distributed among crony politicians, bankers and others and are estimated to exceed revenues from Mexico's principal export (oil), are not reported at all.

The poorest households dispose of a reduced share of income that, in any case, is growing little or not at all in real terms. One result is the generation of new forms and conditions of poverty and social exclusion that have even reached well into the middle classes. In fact, a striking characteristic of imperial-induced inequality is the growth of the urban poor and the changing class composition of the poor: the new poverty is urban rather than rural and extends well beyond the working and producing classes into the once proud but now decimated middle class.

While rural poverty continues to be the rule, the fastest growing number of poor today is found in the cities. The new urban poor are not simply rural migrants but include socially excluded and downwardly mobile workers and lower middle-class individuals who have been fired from their jobs and have found employment in the burgeoning informal sector. The growing armies of urban poor in Latin America now constitute a second and third generation of workers, many of whom live in slums or shantytowns, unable to follow the earlier generations' occupational ladder towards incremental improvement.

One consequence of this class situation has been the skyrocketing growth of crime directly linked to family disintegration and concentrated among young people, who earlier would have channelled their grievances through trade unions or the factory system.

Pillars of Social Exclusion

It has become fashionable to write of the urban poor as "socially excluded" rather than as poor (Pochmann et al., 2004). Not only is this new language more acceptable to the poor, who do not like to see themselves as such, but it is more convenient for the development agencies that have sprung up all over the urban landscape. The term "socially excluded" draws attention away from social relations of capitalist exploitation and oppression, which are associated with or dictate more organized forms of class action. For whatever reason, the conditions of social exclusion, which certainly includes low income and poverty, are more amenable to redress and provoke less violent political responses than relations and conditions of economic exploitation. A probable reason for this is that it is politically more feasible to design more socially inclusive strategies of poverty reduction/alleviation than to directly challenge the existing highly concentrated structure of economic power.

In fact, it is possible, if not necessary or politically expedient, to conceive of the poor as both economically exploited and socially excluded. Needless to say, the social conditions of exploitation derive from the capital-labour relation, which, despite the transformative change in associated conditions of work and forms of employment — in the growth of the so-called "informal sector" over the 1980s and 1990s — still defines the class situation of many if not most urban dwellers. First, urban workers in the so-called informal sector of economically marginal enterprises (street work "on one's own account," to use the language of statisticians) are by no means disconnected from the capitalist system. In effect, they, like the unemployed and rural-to-urban migrants more generally, constitute an enormous reservoir of surplus labour for capital — what Marx in a different historical context termed an "industrial reserve army." This reserve army helps keep down the wages of workers in the formal sector of capitalist enterprise and foreign investment. And it also serves to weaken labour in its capacity to negotiate collective agreements and organize.

Six major "pillars" or structural conditions have been identified as constituting social exclusion[3] (Paugam, 1996):

- dispossession of the means of social production, reflected in the widespread condition of landlessness and near-landlessness and the process of rural outmigration;
- lack of access to urban and rural labour markets and opportunities for wage employment, reflected in the low rate of labour force par-

ticipation and the high rate of unemployment in the rural sector;

- lack of access to good quality or decent jobs, reflected in increased rates of super- and under-employment and in the growth and prevalence of jobs that are contingent in form (seasonal, involuntary part-time, short-term, etc.) with a high degree of informality and inordinately low wages and other forms of remuneration;
- reduced access to government social services in areas of social development such as education, health and social security;
- lack of access to stable forms of adequate income, reflected in the incapacity of many households to meet their basic needs and in indicators of relative and absolute poverty[4]; and, above all,
- exclusion from the apparatus of decision-making or political power, reflected in the centralized nature of the power structure, elite control of the structure, the prevalence of client-patron relations in the political arena and frequent recourse to political organization and action in the form of anti-systemic social movements.

A New Dualism

Presidents Carlos Menem, Fernando Cardoso, Ernesto Zedillo and Eduardo Frei at one time or another all announced the entrance of their respective countries (Argentina, Brazil, Mexico, Chile) into the First World. They showcased modern shopping malls, a boom in cellular phones, supermarkets loaded with imported foods, streets choked with cars and stock markets that attracted big overseas speculators. Today, 15–20 percent of Latin Americans share a First World lifestyle: they send their kids to private schools; belong to private country clubs where they swim, play tennis and do aerobic exercises; get facelifts at private clinics; travel in luxury cars on private toll roads; and communicate via computer, fax and private courier services. They live in gated communities protected by private police. They frequently vacation and shop in New York, Miami, London and Paris. Their children attend overseas universities. They enjoy easy access to influential politicians, media moguls, celebrities and business consultants. They are usually fluent in English and have most of their savings in overseas accounts or in dollar-denominated local paper. They form part of the international circuit of the new imperial system. They are the audience to which presidents address their grandiloquent discourse of a new wave of global prosperity based on an adjustment to the requirements of the new world economic order. Despite the ups and downs of the economy they substantially benefit from the imperial system.

The rest of the population lives in a totally different world. Cuts in social spending and the elimination of basic food subsidies have pushed peasants towards malnutrition and hunger. Large-scale redundancy of factory workers and their entry into the informal sector means a subsistence existence and dependence on the extended family, community-based charities and soup kitchens for survival. Slashed public health and education budgets have resulted in increasing payments and deteriorating services. Cuts in funds for maintenance of water, sewage and other public services have fostered a resurgence of infectious diseases. Declining standards measured in income and living conditions is the reality for two-thirds or more of the population. They have experienced a decline from Third World welfarism to Fourth World immiseration.

As the crisis of the system as a whole deepens, the elite classes intensify the exploitation of wage labour. As the costs of associating with First World powers increases, the elite diverts a greater percentage of state revenues towards subsidizing their partnerships at the expense of social programs for working families. As debt payments accumulate, and interest, royalty and profits move outward, declining incomes shrink the domestic market. Bankruptcies multiply and competition for disappearing overseas markets intensifies. The crises become systemic and economies totter on the verge of collapse. Stagnation turns into depression, and major banks and financial institutions go bankrupt, fuse or are bought by overseas financial groups. Overseas speculators threaten a fast exit. International bailouts to prevent imminent collapse become larger and more frequent.

The Economics of Poverty and the Poverty of Economics

By the end of the 1980s, it was apparent that the neoliberal agenda of policy reform and structural adjustment was very problematic — dysfunctional in economic terms and politically unsustainable or "ungovernable." The problem, as diagnosed early on by Ethan Kapstein (1996), director at the time of the U.S. Council on Foreign Relations (CFR), was that the social inequalities generated and exacerbated by the World Bank's pro-growth policies generates forces of resistance that tend to destabilize the regimes pressured by the World Bank and the IMF to toe the line of structural reform.

The response of the architects of the new world order was fourfold: (1) structural adjustment with a human face in the form of a new social policy (NSP) that targets the poor and seeks to alleviate the dire poverty generated in the adjustment process; (2) the arranged marriage between the forces of economic and political liberalization — capitalism (the free market) and democracy (free elections); (3) a good governance regime in the form of the participation of civil society in the implementation of public policy, via decentralization of decision-making and responsibilities; and (4) a local development strategy based on the accumulation of the poor's social capital — capital embedded and invested in relations of reciprocal exchange and social solidarity (the new paradigm). This local development strategy, implemented with the assistance of NGOs, strategic partners in a program of assistance, was designed to turn social organizations in the popular sector of civil society away from a confrontational approach — direct actions against the government's neoliberal policies — and towards seeking improvements in their lives on the basis of self-development, via support of their micro-enterprises within the local spaces available within the power structure (Harris, 2001; Petras and Veltmeyer, 2005).

Poverty as Global: The Social Dimensions of an Economic and Political Problem

The World Bank discovered the existence of world poverty under the presidency of Robert McNamara, who had just been reassigned by President Johnson from prosecuting the Vietnam War to the war on world poverty. By the calculations of the Bank, at least one fifth of the world population at the time was poor, i.e., unable to meet their basic needs, and about half of these were desperately poor, deprived of their basic needs to the point of seriously affecting their health and survival and certainly reducing life expectation and increasing child and infant mortality, cutting off at the very outset the possibility for the human development of a large part of the world's poor.

In 1982, at the onset of the debt crisis in Latin America and Sub-Saharan Africa, close to 40 percent of the population in Latin America, which had experienced several decades of economic growth and social development, was deemed to be poor, with the highest incidence and worst conditions found in rural society (Jazairy, Alamgir and Panuccio, 1992). By the end of the decade, however, after several years of experience with the new economic model of free market structural reforms, the rate of poverty, as calculated by ECLAC and defined by a basic subsistence income (poverty line), had increased to 44 percent — a rate if anything higher than in 1973 when the problem was first diagnosed by World Bank economists. Fifteen years later, in 2005, after two decades of what the World Bank describes as "pro-poor policies," the problem of poverty is as visible as ever, notwithstanding the Bank's efforts at reducing the rate of poverty by changing the definition. Even by the World Bank's highly conservative and very problematic new measure (the number of households subsisting on less than $2 a day), the world's poor had dramatically increased in number if not as a percentage of the total population. If one were to use a more conventional and valid measure of poverty (the income needed by individuals or households to access adequate goods and services to meet their basic needs), then the poor as a percentage of the population and as a social group would be considerably larger.

The number of poor today represent virtually the same rate (percentage of the total population) as in 1989, when the World Bank began in earnest its anti-poverty campaign. Indeed the evidence suggests that, not only has the international development community failed to reduce the incidence of poverty or even to substantially alleviate its worst effects, but the World Bank's pro-poor policies actually generated new forms of poverty, extending it from the countryside into the urban centres. In the 1980s, the bulk of the poor were found in the rural areas of society, victims of an economic and social structure that was entrenched in hundreds of years of exploitation, social exclusion, oppression and discrimination.

Towards the end of the 1990s, as a fairly direct result of neoliberal policies and a massive rural-to-urban migration, poverty increasingly assumed an urban form. In the case of Argentina, it has been estimated by government officials that up to half of the new poor originated not in the countryside but in a hitherto powerful and sizeable middle class. The other half of the poor originated in the low income sectors of the working class — the working poor, the self-employed, the unemployed and underemployed, and the vast mass of street workers that make up the informal sector.

The World Bank on Growth and Poverty Reduction: Distribution Matters
Economists at the World Bank have carried on with little respite and no fundamental change in policy a three-decades-long war on poverty, and with it an equally protracted debate on the relation of economic growth to social inequality — and more recently on the effect of the World Bank's structural adjustment program on social inequalities in income distribution. In the 1970s, the orthodoxy of development economics was that a growth-first approach that relied on the market for the distribution of income could not resolve the problem of poverty. The dominant theory at the time was that the reduction/alleviation of poverty would require the efforts of an active developmental state in redistributing market-generated inequalities in income distribution, i.e., a growth-with-equity or income redistribution approach.

However, this social welfare approach was seriously contested by economists armed with a neoclassical theory of economic growth. In this view, which came into its own in the 1980s in the context of a conservative reaction and neoliberal revolution, the market, liberated from government constraint, was the most efficient mechanism for an optimum allocation of resources across the world system. From this neoliberal perspective, government income-redistribution programs, via progressive taxation, at best were ineffectual and at worst seriously interfered with the proper functioning of the free market.

This view would prevail throughout the 1980s, until widespread evidence that a growth-only approach (free market policy reforms) and a process of structural adjustment were socially and politically unsustainable, generating as they did destabilizing forms of social discontent; even worse these policies proved to be economically dysfunctional, failing to deliver on the expectation of economic growth. With the evidence in, and after an exceedingly long process of transition, a number of economists once again began to rethink the link between growth (and pro-growth policies) and social inequality (and poverty). The evidence in this reassessment appears to be mixed and there

43

certainly is no new consensus. But a number of economists, even those at the World Bank, established as an indisputable fact that a free market, pro-growth approach (and corresponding policies) seriously exacerbated existing social inequalities without any appreciable economic or social benefits. On the contrary, the reluctant conclusion drawn from unavoidable and pressing facts was that improved access by the poor to society's productive resources (such as land, capital and technology) and greater equity in the distribution of income were needed to allow for and promote a process of economic and social development (Birdsall, 1997).

It was further argued by these revisionist economists that the market by itself could not be counted on for creating these preconditions; it required corrective action by the state — in effect, restoring (at least in theory) a policy of mixed support for the market and an active state. Although this view was adopted by an increasing number of economists at the Bank (for example, Stiglitz), it did not affect the Bank's fundamental commitment to macroeconomic (structural) and political reform — to its "pro-growth" "pro-poor" policies [5] (Eastwood and Lipton, 2001; Kakwani and Pernia, 2000).

Back to the War on Poverty

No problem describes so well international development as a project taken on by the world community of developed nations as poverty, the problem that is defined most often in socioeconomic terms as the inability of a given population to meet its basic needs. The World Bank in particular took on this project in 1973, when, under Robert McNamara's presidency, it discovered that at a minimum two-fifths of the world's population was unable to meet its basic needs and this because of a fundamental lack of income — a problem it would come to define as "low income countries." Over the years, the Bank has periodically reaffirmed its commitment in this regard, declaring war against it in late 1988 in the context of Sub-Saharan Africa and more generally in its 1980 *World Development Report*, and then again most recently in the late 1990s, when the Bank defined its mission in terms of the on-going (for some decades by then) war against poverty.

So where do we (i.e., the world and the Bank) stand today after so many battles staged and fought, so many diverse strategies pursued with so much money and passion (see the Bank's masthead mission statement), so much effort all targeted at the poor?

We stand exactly where we were in the 1970s and in a number of ways further back. Not only have the numbers of the poor increased, with no change in the percentage of the population affected by poverty in its various dimensions and perverse effects, but it has taken on new forms, reaching even into the households of what had hitherto been the middle class in terms of income. In 1973 the poor were some 40 percent of the total population; in 1983, after a decade of liberal reforms aimed by governments at redistributing

44

market-generated incomes, the rate of poverty if anything had increased. By 1993, a decade into a regional and world-wide debt crisis and widespread implementation of a neoliberal approach towards development, most people in the world's poor countries were in as bad a situation or worse off. Three decades of a concerted war, with countless battles waged at the national and local levels, and no development whatsoever — no change and no improvement.

This fact begs several questions. One is about the strategy and tactics used to wage this war — its weapons. Perhaps the weapons were faulty or inadequate. Or poorly targeted. Or, more likely, used in a misguided and faulty campaign, marred by misguided strategy and inappropriate, ineffective tactics. Even more likely is that the war was fought with mistaken ideas as to the causes of the problem. Practice, as we know, closely follows theory. The question is: what strategies have been pursued in the war against poverty? And what theory or assumptions lie behind them?

The World Bank's first anti-poverty approach, in the 1970s, was based on the notion that every individual had certain definable basic needs that have to be met in order to reach a minimally acceptable level of what would later be dubbed "human development." The defined minimum included access to a quota of nutrition and food security, access to potable water, adequate shelter, protection from disease, a minimum level of schooling, some level of personal security and decency. Beyond these basic needs, theorists (mostly economists), in their consultations with and advice to the World Bank and governments, varied in their advice and prescriptions, with lists of needs that included political participation and, in one case (see Max-Neef, Elizalde and Hopenhayen, 1965), up to twenty-two needs (conditions for humans to realize their potential) with their identified corresponding "satisfiers." These same economists devised strategies based on this conception of poverty as relative or absolute deprivation, low income and the lack of access to essential services. The most common strategies were income redistribution (growth with redistribution); governments were advised to implement social programs (education, health, social welfare and security) and programs of integrated rural development (subsidized credit, etc.), funded via mechanisms such as progressive taxation on earned and investment income. These development and social programs were more or less implemented within the framework of macroeconomic policies of a state-led model of economic development.

By 1983, it was clear that income redistribution strategies had dismally failed to close the income gap, and many liberal reformers lost confidence in their ideas and policy prescriptions, creating a space that a new generation of policy advisors (many connected to the World Bank and the IMF) soon filled with different ideas and prescriptions based on a neoclassical theory of economic development aligned with a new economic model. Within

45

this new policy framework, the war on poverty was recommenced through structural adjustment, a program of market-friendly macroeconomic policy reforms. These policies were (and still are) deemed to be absolutely minimum conditions for reactivating the economy with pro-growth and thus pro-poor policies (World Bank, 2004a). These pro-growth policies, implemented at the national level by the governments of the day, were described by the Bank as the minimum policy and institutional framework for attacking the problem at the sub-national and local levels via a program of self-help projects — engaging the poor themselves in the process as partners as well as participants, and enlisting the help of the NGOs (World Bank, 2004b).

In the 1990s, the apparent intractability of the poverty problem led the Bank (and its strategic partners, particularly in the U.N.) to enlist the help of the private sector (profit-oriented enterprises as well as business associations) and to modify its approach towards poverty eradication/reduction/alleviation. Globalization was retained as the best means of creating general prosperity, and the new economic model of structural reform was retained as the fundamental macroeconomic policy framework (pro-growth = pro-poor). But within this institutional and policy framework, adjusted and tweaked for greater functionality and sustainability (adding to it a new social policy that protected the most vulnerable, providing them a minimal level of economic and social security), the war against poverty was prosecuted with a much greater reliance on full participation of the poor themselves. The poor were helped to enhance their capacity for economic and social development and empowered to find their own solutions to the problem of poverty (with development assistance from the Bank and other overseas development associations).

Within this reformulated framework (pro-poor institutions and policies) various poverty reduction/alleviation strategies were designed. The most popular, perhaps, in regard to rural poor and their communities, was the "sustainable livelihoods approach" — a school of development thought and practice that emphasizes the critical role of social capital, building on assets that the poor are deemed to have in abundance. Hitherto, development theory and practice had always emphasized financial and physical forms of capital as the critical ingredients of the development process. However, improving access to the resources had proven to be difficult if not impossible; there were too many obstacles to overcome — e.g., political opposition from the proprietors of land and capital, owners of the means of production, whose rights of ownership were protected by private property legal regimes.

The advantage of the social capital approach towards economic and social development — in alleviating, if not eradicating or reducing, poverty — was that it did not require or entail fundamental economic change and state-led social reform. It only required the full participation of the poor themselves, with minimum technical and financial assistance from the outside. It did not presume a structural source of widespread poverty (lack of access to productive resources — financial and physical capital, land, etc.). Nor did it view the World Bank's macroeconomic policies as a major contributing factor to poverty, a major structural obstacle to its remediation. Poverty here was viewed primarily as a matter of (1) social exclusion (a problem that could be remedied without fundamental structural change); (2) inadequate support of needed structural reforms, or no will to stay the course; (3) failure to take advantage of existing opportunities for development in the world economy; and (4) various deficiencies in the local society and economies (corrupt officials, rentierism, lack of entrepreneurship, ineffective policy framework, inappropriate politics, orientation towards traditional non-modern values, etc.).

The problem for the Bank was how to implement its structural reform policies without provoking destabilizing demands for fundamental change. In other words, the problem, as the Bank itself has admitted, is essentially political: how to convince policy-makers and politicians to stay the course of pro-growth policy reforms in an environment of growing political opposition and resistance. On this the World Bank's position is fairly clear. In the words of the "Economic Focus" editorial writer for *The Economist* (22 September, 2005), "The World Bank cannot go where its research is leading it," namely the recognition that economic and political elites in many parts of the world "protect their interest and hold down the poor."

Within the framework of the Bank's own pro-poor macroeconomic policies, a partnership approach towards local community-based development plus support for a social capital approach, and an appeal in favour of the forces of economic and political freedom, the World Bank added its own twist to what it regards as best practice in its fight against poverty. In the late 1990s, economists at the Bank conceived of a "Poverty Reduction Strategy Paper" (PRSP) approach, in which, in exchange for future assistance, governments in the developing world of poor countries would sign on to the Bank's fight against poverty — a coalition of the willing, able and desperate.

The Social and Political Dynamics of Income Distribution

Critical features of any state are their regimes of (capital) accumulation and distribution, and their effective articulation. In the post–Second World War context, regimes of distribution were constituted by the Keynesian state in the First World of Western Europe and North America; the socialist state in the Second World of the Soviet Union and Eastern Europe; and the developmental state of the Third World. However, toward the end of the 1970s, a worldwide accumulation crisis created conditions for a neoliberal regime of accumulation based on foreign investment: the state, in effect, withdrew from its responsibility to secure an effective form of social distribution, leaving this responsibility to civil society, in effect, leaving people to fend for themselves (in adjusting to, managing and resisting the forces of globalization) but also, as an unintended but inescapable consequence, generating the conditions of a distributional crisis. This crisis, as Rapley (2004) argues, is bringing about the demise of neoliberalism and its foreign investment regime.

Systemic responses to the distributional crisis have included attempts, at times successful and mostly ineffective, to manage the explosive forces of political resistance. Another response has been to redesign the structural adjustment program of reform, providing for a new social policy targeted at the poor, so as to give the whole reform process a human face. And a third systemic response, another element of a post–Washington Consensus, has been to establish a more ostensibly democratic form of governance — self-management of the distributional crisis. The end result is an emerging political crisis: an explosion of local, regional and sub-national conflicts over society's productive resources that have exceeded the capacity of a decentralized state to control or manage.

Conclusion

The available evidence suggests that both social inequality and poverty are intricately, if indirectly, linked to the pro-growth, pro-poor imperialist policies of the World Bank. A second, incontrovertible, fact is that a foreign investment regime, promoted by policies of financial liberalization, privatization and market deregulation, exacerbates these inequalities and in the process generates a wide array of disabling social problems, conditions of low income and impoverishment, such as disease, malnutrition, high levels of child mortality and widespread social disorganization. In fact, foreign investment provides a link between neoliberalism and structural adjustment on the one hand and social inequality and poverty on the other.

The link is in the outflow of capital — the transfer to the centre of the world capitalist system resources that were generated on its periphery — resources that constitute a potential source of capital, which instead of being invested productively, are siphoned off. In effect, foreign investment, via the operations of the multinationals, create a paradoxical situation of capital shortage. Thus the myth is sustained that peripheral economies are underdeveloped because of a shortage of financial resources and the lack of an institutional capacity to exploit and develop these scarce resources, and to access foreign capital. Foreign investors and MNCs, parading as white knights bearing much needed capital, technological and managerial knowhow and jobs, in reality serve as a mechanism of imperial domination, capitalist underdevelopment, technological dependence and capital drain — an enormous economic cost relative to the meagre economic benefits provided by foreign investments.

Another conclusion that can be drawn from the pattern of developments associated with the North-South transfer of financial resources is that the economic costs of foreign investment, substantial as they are, pale in significance compared to the heavy and widespread social costs and the negative impact on the livelihoods and the social existence of people living and working in the popular sector of developing societies. Widespread poverty and a deepening of social inequalities in access to world society's productive resources and income are the indirect result of foreign investment — of the policies and conditions created as means of facilitating the entry of foreign capital.

Finally, neither the politics of adjustment nor those of resistance have been able to bring about any substantive change in the workings of neoliberalism. Nor has politics in one form or another been able to stave off the impending crisis of global capitalism, the victim of its own contradictions. As for the war on poverty, the major response of the system to offset these contradictions by alleviating their effects, it is nothing more than a palliative, providing relief to the poor while continuing to promote policies that benefit the rich and super-rich. The super-rich are no longer regarded as "the greedy devourers of the substance of the poor, the ugly monopolists of resources" (Seabrook, 2006). No longer the exploiters and bloodsuckers of capitalist lore, they have been turned into philanthropists, the "virtuous possessors of fabulous fortunes by whose grace and charity alone the dire poverty of the destitute will be relieved" (ibid).

Notes

1. According to the latest U.S. Census Report (August 2005), the years 2000 to 2004 witnessed marked advances in the degree of social inequality in the distribution of wealth and income, with a corresponding growth of wealth at one extreme and poverty at the other. The richest 10 percent of households, it appears, garnered almost all of the new wealth generated over the years in question. As for the poor, their number has increased each year, growing from 35.9 million in 2003 to 37 million in 2004 (DPA, AFP y Reuters, Washington, DC, 31 August 2005). The U.S. Census Office also reports on the ethnic or racial dimension of poverty. Within the Hispanic population, now making up over a third of the total U.S. population, the rate of poverty has remained relatively stable at 21.9 percent, twice the rate of non-Hispanic whites. As for the black population, the poverty rate also remained about the same, at 24.7 percent or triple the poverty rate of non-Hispanic whites. Given the relative stability of the poverty rates within the Hispanic and black populations, the relative growth in the number of the poor over the past four years has been particularly pronounced within the dominant working-class white population, a phenomenon with presumed political implications.

2. This restrictive policy on capital outflows bears comparison to the Draconian controls imposed by the Government of South Korea on domestic investors in

the mid-1990s. According to Chang and Grabel (2004: 133), it was this policy that saved South Korea from a debt crisis despite its having become at the time the fourth largest foreign debtor in the world.

3. Given the array of international organizations and research institutions, both within the U.N. system and the international development community, involved in the war against poverty and the broader conditions of social exclusion, it is clear that the problem has not only reached critical proportions but that it is global in scope. One of many organizations set up in the search for solutions to the problem of social exclusion is the Research Centre for Analysis of Social Exclusion (CASE), established in October 1997 at the London School of Economics and Political Science (LSE) with funding from the U.K. Economic and Social Research Council.

4. A poverty-oriented "basic needs" approach dominated the study of international development in the 1970s. This originated in the 1973 discovery by the World Bank that upwards of two-fifths of the world's population was in a state of relative deprivation, unable to meet their basic needs. According to Amartya Sen, a household without sufficient income to meet the basic needs of its members is poor, a condition that can be measured in terms of a head count, that is, the number and percentage of the population that falls below a defined income poverty line or, according to Sen, by an index of disparity in income distribution, viz. income gap ratio multiplied by the number of the poor, which provides a coefficient of specific poverty.

5. The tortuous efforts of the World Bank economists to square this circle — to place the peg of "pro-poor" policies in the square of "pro-growth" policies of market-led or -friendly structural reform — can be traced out in the various websites and electronic discussion groups on pro-poor policies (poverty reduction/alleviation) set up by the Bank <www.worldbank.org>.

Chapter 3

Social Capital and Local Development
A New Paradigm?

A spectre is haunting the study of development: the search for a new paradigm. This search can be traced through twists and turns in both the theory and practice of development since the mid-1970s. The first critical turn in the now widespread effort to construct a new paradigm relates to a crisis in the dominant form of analysis — structuralism — used in the construction of development theory and an associated failure to conceptualize and theorize the role of culture and ideology in the development process. This crisis was reflected in and led to a "theoretical impasse" and new ways of thinking and forms of analysis based on a postmodernist and postdevelopment perspective on society and development (Schuurman, 1993). The second impetus for constructing a new paradigm was a widely perceived absence in development theory of "the social," the conditions of which were abstracted from analysis in the dominant paradigm. The third critical factor was a counter-revolution in development theory and practice associated with a new economic model (neoliberal capitalist development and globalization). This model aimed to construct a global economy based on a new world order in which the factors and agents of economic growth are liberated from the regulatory and other constraints of the nation-state. I argue that the conditions generated in this process of structural adjustment to the requirements of the new world order created the impetus to a process of local development and a revival of a community development movement based on the accumulation of social capital.

To all appearances, the efforts to establish a local form of development arises from a concern for a more participatory approach that is not only socially inclusive, equitable and sustainable, and initiated from below and within civil society, but empowering of the individuals involved, particularly the poor themselves (Bebbington et al., 2006; Veltmeyer and O'Malley, 2001). But it could be argued that a social capital focus on local development has little to do with a popular movement for social change and much more to do with a well-defined strategy, pursued by the World Bank and other international organizations in the development project, to turn people at the grassroots away from a politics of confrontation and direct action against the structures of political and economic power and to opt instead to seek improvements within the local spaces of this structure. This is to say — and I argue — that the recent and widespread resort to the concept of social capital by the "development community" in both academic and policy-making circles, and the entire local development agenda, has an ideological and political significance. The aim of this chapter is to establish this significance.

The Local and the Social in the Development Process

The search for a new paradigm can be traced back to the 1970s, but it acquired a particular vigour and a very broad scope in the 1980s in the context of a turn in the mainstream of development thinking and practice towards a new economic model that prioritized the free market as opposed to the developmental state (Bulmer-Thomas, 1996). The search for "another development" sought to move beyond both the market and the state and the debates that surrounded and still surround the state-market relation within the development process. The proponents of another development visualized it in terms of the agency of community-based or local development, reaching beyond both the state and the market into communities, particularly those with marginal status, in an unfolding process of globalization and structural adjustment. The aim of theorists and practitioners in the mould of this new approach was to advance an alternative form of development that was more humane in form and scale, sustainable in terms of the environment and livelihoods, socially inclusive and equitable, and participatory — initiated "from below" and "from within" civil society and not "from above" (government) and "from outside" (international assistance).

Writing about a "paradigmatic shift" and the need to construct a "new paradigm" has dominated development discourse since the mid-1970s, but it was given a major impetus in the following decade by a widely perceived "theoretical impasse" arising from forms of structuralism and associated meta-theories of capitalist development, industrialization and modernization (Veltmeyer, 2002). To some extent this paradigm shift has to with a longstanding concern to give development a social dimension. Since it emerged as a project and field of study, development had been dominated by economics. Development economists abstracted the social and the political treating them as externalities, from a process that was based on an analysis of strictly economic factors. However, in the 1970s, this approach gave way to efforts to conceptualize the role and weight of the social in an analysis of the development process. One of these efforts was in regard to the concept of "capital," which was central to an analysis of the dynamics of economic growth. It was theorized that economic growth and associated national development hinged on a process of capital accumulation, which in turn was dependent on the rate at which national income was saved and productively invested. Capital in this process was conceived of primarily in financial (money) and physical (technology) terms as assets or productive resources.

It was in this context that the search for another development emerged. First, development was viewed broadly and analyzed in terms of its social conditions, including health and education. Second, development, as the accumulation of society's productive resources, was analyzed in terms of the diverse forms — natural, physical and financial, and, by extension, social and political — taken by capital. The concept of "social capital," defined as the norms, institutions and organizations that promote trust and cooperation among persons in communities and in the wider society, was initially advanced by several sociologists (Coleman and Bourdieu) but was then elaborated on by leading development economists such as Chambers (1983) and Putnam (1993, 2000, 2002). At issue here was their search for a new paradigm — an alternative way of thinking about development and translating theory into practice (Durston, 1999: 104).

That was then (the 1980s) and this is now (a new millennium). We are on the verge of a new paradigm, within which it is claimed that stable relationships based on trust, cooperation and norms of reciprocal (as opposed to money) exchange can reduce "transaction costs," produce "public goods," facilitate the "constitution of sound civil societies," empower and constitute people as "social actors" and, above all, promote development at the community level, thereby reducing/ameliorating the socioeconomic (and psychological) conditions of poverty. The social capital paradigm aims to be a unified theory, incorporating concepts from different fields — reciprocity, social networks, participatory development and governance — and strengthening civil society and the dynamics of participatory development based on resources that the poor have in abundance.

Robert Putnam's book, *Making Democracy Work* (1993), by some accounts, served as a major catalyst for generating widespread interest in social capital as a research and policy tool. But the rapid spread and ubiquity of this notion of social capital in academe and its wide-ranging applications in research, policy-formulation and practice have given rise to serious questioning. First, what is striking about social capital are not only the extent of its influence and the speed with which this has been achieved but also its ready and enthusiastic acceptance by both scholars and policy-makers. These features are aptly captured by the World Bank's notion of social capital as "the glue that holds society together" and, as such, the "missing link" in an analysis of the development process (Harris and de Renzio, 1997; Solow, 2000).

Second, despite the plethora of survey articles that litters the intellectual landscape, the concept is notoriously difficult to define. Most recent contributions to the literature acknowledge this before adding a definition to suit their own purpose (Fine, 2001b). The elusiveness of the notion of social capital is reflected in the not infrequent suggestion that it is merely a metaphor or heuristic device. This is even more so in the inverted logic of World Bank projects that define social capital in the process of measuring it — as Fine (2001b: 11–15) notes, "to have what it is confused with what it does," and, in the process, "to be subject to perverse, dark, negative and down-sides." As Portes (1998) points out, the World Bank's logic here is anything but clear, caught up as it is in a vicious circle of tautological reasoning, without any basis in empirical fact.

Third, the concept is used to describe virtually anything from the networks formed by the poor, the sick, the criminal and the corrupt to the social dynamics of the (dys)functional family, schooling, community development, work and organization, democracy and governance, collective action, the intangible assets of the social economy, "the analysis and promotion of peasant-level development" or, indeed, any aspect of social, cultural and economic activity across time and place — everything, it would seem, except the norms, institutions and social networks formed by those that constitute what Salbuchi (2000) terms the "braintrust of the world," the class that runs the global economy and makes up its rules.

The final concern about social capital is in regard to its ideological uses and political implications. What appears to be is missing in the analysis is any concern with the institutionality of economic and political power. Social capital appears to serve analysts and policy-makers in the same way that post-modern social theory serves social analysis — a means of eluding what for most people is all too real: the dynamic workings of the capitalist system in its economic and political dimensions and global extension. In the process, the social dynamics of the power relations that define (and determine in reality if not in thought) life for most people are inverted: what is essentially a class struggle over state and economic power materializes as "empowerment" — a sense of participation in decisions that affect one's life and livelihood without the need to change *in reality* the operating structures of the "system." To invert the maxim established by Marx, the point here is not to *change* the world but to *reinterpret* it — to change oneself (to think and feel differently, more positively, about the world and oneself) rather than the system.

Another dimension of this criticism is that the concept of social capital, in its use as a research and policy tool, is ideologically too convenient. Harris's (2001) argument and that of others in this connection makes three points. One is that making people responsible for their own development falsely implies that they are responsible for their problems, such as poverty, drawing attention away from the operating structures of the economic and social system. In its broad focus on the dynamics of civil society, social capital ignores (abstracts from the analysis) the dynamics associated with the formal structures and institutions of society's political economy, particularly that of state power. A second line of criticism is that in its application the concept of social capital is both immobilizing and demobilizing regarding social change. Development takes the form of seeking to make improvements within the local spaces of this structure, and doing so on the basis of very limited resources, rather than challenging this structure or demanding improved access to more critical or important productive resources such as land (and related natural resources), capital in the form of credit) and technology. Ownership and control of these resources remain concentrated in the hands (and institutions) of the rich and powerful while the poor and powerless are encouraged to exploit their own rather limited resources and to do so without challenging the holders of economic and political power. Some critics here talk of participatory development and social capital as illusory, implying not so much that social capital is based on false assumptions or "unrealistic expectations" — the most common criticism — as that it takes away from people their intellectual and political tools for bringing about change.

This chapter elaborates on this last point before proceeding to deconstruct the concept of social capital from a critical perspective. The objective is, in part, to explain the fascination of so many policy-makers and analysts with the concept of social capital and, in part, to deconstruct the political effects of an analysis based on the concept of social capital. The concern is not so much to seek the putative motivation behind the fascination with and uses of the social capital concept as to identify its deleterious effects in analysis and politics.

Making Democracy Work: Putnam on Social Capital

The concept of social capital has been around for much longer than Putnam's 1993 book. The work of Coleman, Bourdieu and other foundational authors of the social capital paradigm (see Baron, Field and Schuller, 2000, for a review) preceded its publication by years. However, Putnam's book catapulted the concept of social capital to centre stage of an extraordinary range of research and policy agendas in the area of community development. Putnam defines social capital in terms of the community cohesion associated with the existence of cooperative and accessible community networks/organizations; high levels of participation in these networks; a strong sense of local identity; and high levels of trust, relations of reciprocal exchange and solidarity amongst members of the community. The World Bank and the Inter-American Development Bank (IDB) in their respective websites and many studies on the theme — see also ECLAC — have stayed close to this definition, viewing social capital through the lens of social networks as a resource that can be mobilized in the direction of poverty reduction and good governance (Rao, 2002; Solow, 2000).

In the form adopted by the World Bank and most other development agencies, i.e., as a resource for self-help (development from below and within), social capital can be used to predict and explain a wide range of outcomes, including those related to household income in Tanzania and the Philippines; the effectiveness of local governments in Italy, the U.S. and elsewhere ("making democracy work"); the complex dynamics of community-based, peasant or indigenous development; and, of course, the best way to bring about poverty reduction and relief, the Bank's institutional mandate and agenda. The concept has also become the darling of high profile researchers in the development field and a host of influential policy-makers and development agencies from the World Bank and the IDB to ECLAC and the UNDP. Each of these agencies has set up within its organization a division dedicated to the advancement of social capital and has sponsored workshops and publications, including practitioner and policy-making guides.

Shortly after its appearance, a leading international journal reviewed Putnam's work and cited his book, *Making Democracy Work*, as "the greatest work of social science since Marx and Pareto" — an overstatement to be sure but a clear reflection of the enormous interest that the concept of social capital would attract. The why of the excitement is difficult to determine, but there is no question that the high level of interest in the concept among academics, policy-makers and practitioners coincided with the resurgence of the community development movement, which had been on the wane since the mid- to late 1960s, when it withered on the vine of the popular state-led model of economic development. The increasing use of social capital theory also coincided with a neoconservative impulse to downsize the state and take it out of the economy, and a concomitant concern with the constitution and strengthening of civil society.

The intellectual context of this interest in democratizing the relation of the state to civil society was the search for an alternative form of development that was participatory and empowering, initiated from below (and within) civil society, equitable and socially inclusive, sustainable in terms of livelihoods as well as the environment and, above all, based on the poor's own agency. The World Bank added a twist on this search for another development — a new paradigm that placed people at the centre of the development enterprise — by designing a program of structural reforms in government policy designed to provide the poor and powerless (as well as the rich and powerful) "freedom of choice" and "the ability to shape their own lives" (Narayan, 2002).

Another contextual element was the emergence of a concern to democratize the state and to engage civil society in the construction of a decentralized good governance regime (Bardhan, 1997; Blair, 1997; UNDP, 1996). Civil society organizations (CSOs), formed in what was once termed "the third sector," were assigned the lead role in a process of political (democratic) and economic (alternative) development, actively participating in the implementation, if not design, of economic, social and political development projects and in the construction of public policy (at least in ensuring transparency and the accountability of public decision-makers).

Studies by Rondinelli, Nellis and Cheema (1983) on government decentralization helped establish this shift in development and political thinking within the global network of development agencies and governments that assumed both responsibility for and a leading role in the construction of a new world order. At issue was a concern for the "politics of adjustment" — ensuring the stability of regimes committed to the new economic model as the only means of paving the way forward towards prosperity and, as the Bank saw (and continues to see) it, the best way to fight poverty. Democratizing institutional reforms, such as decentralization and the strengthening of civil society *vis-à-vis* government, were viewed as necessary adjuncts to a policy shift towards the free market, liberating it from government interference. The aim was to bring about a marriage of strategic import and political convenience between capitalism and democracy — economic and political liberalization (Dominguez and Lowenthal, 1996). And the key to this marriage was good governance, which required the democratization of relations between the state and civil society, reforming the former, and in regard to the latter, securing its participation in the construction of public policy and government decision-making.

Whatever the merits of Putnam's book it was a book of its time, the widespread interest in it purely a matter of intellectual and political context. And in this case, context was everything. Ben Fine (2001a and b) among many others, have pointed out one reason why the concept of social capital was grasped so enthusiastically: in the absence of any theoretical grounding within a broader theory of power relations, it served as a blank cipher that could be moulded to diverse political agendas. Above all, it allowed for a form of development that did not entail a challenge of the power structure. The advantage of social capital (for the powers that be) is that it is easily accumulated (an asset that the poor are deemed to have in abundance) and effectively mobilized without social change. In terms of development — strictly speaking, social rather than economic — it is limited to the local spaces available within the existing structure of economic and political power. Social change in turn (and development is predicated on change) affects the individuals (presumed beneficiaries, converted into actors) more than the system. It can be implemented without attacking this structure or changing the distribution of natural, physical and financial forms of capital. Theoretical models of development to that point were all predicated on accumulating and mobilizing these forms of capital, a political process fraught with social and political conflict and difficult to implement.

In the context of the sweeping epoch-defining reforms in the early to mid-1980s, the concept of social capital came as something of a gift to thinkers of the neoliberal free market school — proponents of economic and political freedom who argued that grassroots voluntary organizations and neighbourhood networks should take over functions (e.g., welfare, development) previously assigned to governments. The building of social capital was used to justify cuts in welfare spending in more affluent countries and to reduce development aid to poor countries — to make them more self-reliant (an interesting ideological twist on the structuralist notion and ideology of national self-determination). Development, it was widely argued, should be owned by the poor themselves and based on their own agency, rather than relying on outside agents, agencies and resources.

The coincidence of some of Putnam's ideas with the rise of "third way" (centre-right-wing, liberal) politics and the turn of development agencies and governments towards an alternative, more participatory form of development and politics (a new paradigm, in academic discourse) explains the exploding interest in, and use of, the concept of social capital by academics and development practitioners. An interest in, and increasing use of, this concept have unfolded on the centre-right of the ideological-political spectrum, but it also appeals to many on the left. The "new left," defined in social rather than political terms, argue that it is only through the building of social capital that the hitherto excluded will ever gain the confidence or power to lobby governments to meet their needs and to revert their social exclusion. Thus, the building of relations of trust, local identity and neighbourhood networks — an economy of solidarity, as Razeto (1988, 1993) defined it — becomes a new politics for the left, the grist for a new way of doing politics. It also leads more or less directly towards the "anti- or no-power" form of leftist politics that has made such inroads in Latin America (Holloway, 2002). This politics features the avoidance of class struggle for state power and associated confrontational politics.

Social Capital and Its Critics: Unrealistic Expectations or Political Demobilization?

A group of researchers affiliated with the Gender Institute of the London School of Economics (LSE) examined the potential of Putnam's "social capital" for describing local community life in southeast England (Campbell, 2001). They found that the concept would need to be quite dramatically reworked to apply to these small communities. They also found that Putnam's conceptualization of a "cohesive community," characterized by a sense of common identity and generalized trust between neighbourhood residents, bore little resemblance to the rapidly changing, dynamic and divided nature of contemporary community life. For one thing, membership in formal organizations of the type emphasized by Putnam, such as residents associations or church groups, was extremely low, with people's main social networks consisting of informal groups of friends and relatives. In fact, the notion of generalized trust or a common identity with others in the same neighbour- hood seemed rather bizarre to the interview informants, presumed actors in this context of social capital formation. More generally, the researchers on this project found that once they had paid the mortgage and cooked for the children, members of the community had little or no time or interest in community life, in participating in its informal or formal institutions. In short, little evidence was found for the actual or latent culture of community participation presupposed in the concept of social capital.

Not surprisingly, Campbell and her fellow researchers also found that those networks and resources that did exist were not equally created or sus- tained and accessed by everyone in the community. In terms of trust and common identity, the local community was fractured by divisions based on generation, gender and housing tenure, not to mention class (which, as it happens, they did not). These divisions, the authors concluded, rendered impossible a sense of common identity or a belief in the value of coopera- tion or solidarity action with other community members. In other words, they raised the question begged by virtually all community development scholars and practitioners: is there a community at all? Does "community," as presumed or defined by the architects of social capital (as both a problem and a solution), even exist?

This question raises others. Can one meaningfully talk about social capital as the property of spatially located communities without taking account of intra-community differences in the way in which social capital is created, sustained and accessed? Community social capital is a particular form of social capital, which comprises the informal content of institutions that are presumably aimed at "the common good." But what is the common good when civil society is divided and fragmented and members of a particular "community" do not participate equally, if at all, in its institutions? A review of large-scale survey studies that measure aggregate levels of social capital across states or towns, suburbs or communities of one sort or another indicates that they generally ignore social divisions, taking a community of interest and identity for granted. Studies in diverse contexts suggest that more often than not there is no community (*gemeinschaft* in the formulation of Ferdinand Tonnies), only a class- or otherwise socially divided society (*gesellschaft*).

The LSE's Gender Institute found that in the small towns and suburbs they studied, the subjects and objects of their research not only did not constitute themselves as a community but they identified themselves primarily in ethnic terms, as Pakistani, Kashmiri, African-Caribbean, White English, etc., and secondarily in class terms. They also discovered dramatic differences in the way in which different groups created and accessed social capital. In effect, the study found that its subjects-objects occupied a definable location in a social structure but did not in any way constitute a community nor for that matter did all or many of the residents (individuals defined in spatial rather than social terms) participate equally in the same informal institutions. When they did participate — in the family, for example — the institutions involved did not constitute residents as a social network or as members of a particular community with a commonality of interest.

John Durston, Social Affairs officer of ECLAC's Social Development Division, in a review of the social dynamics associated with diverse World Bank and BID (Banco Interamericano de Desarrollo) funded anti-poverty projects, particularly in the empty institutional landscape of eastern Guatemala, made a similar discovery. For example, in regard to the peasant communities covered by the Support Project for Small-scale Producers of Zacapa and Chiquimula, he found that, despite the presence of a "dynamic repertoire of norms" that could support "solidarity and reciprocal practices," community members displayed a relatively individualistic culture of dependence and domination (1999: 103). Significantly, one would presumably expect community spirit and thus social capital to be more easily constructed in rural settings such as presented by Guatemala, Ecuador, Bolivia, Peru and other countries endowed with large or significant indigenous populations and thus the object of "ethnodevelopmen" (World Bank, 1996, 2004b).

Nevertheless, Durston, who, despite his reservations, is committed to social capital as a research and policy tool, argues that "with the recovery of institutional practices of the past" (see the World Bank in its conception of "ethnodevelopment"), "opportunities for developing new group strategies" and "external support and training," it is possible to create social capital in these communities and thus "turn an excluded sector into a social actor on the micro-regional scene" (Durston, 1999: 103). It would appear — from the voluminous literature in this regard — that there is no shortage of development scholars and practitioners taking this line, even though several authors, including Putnam (1993: 184), acknowledge that it is difficult, if not impossible, to create or construct social capital where none exists. In other words, the dominant view is that it is possible (and necessary) is to build on existing reservoirs of social capital — or to "leverage" the social capital available within existing organizations and communities. According to Durston (1999: 115), "reciprocity norms and practices [that usually lead to cooperation] exist in small local groups everywhere [in most modern human cultures]."

As to how to generate, build or leverage social capital the literature is inconclusive (Durston, 1999: 105ff.). The one area of agreement is that the constructability of social capital is based on a commonality of interest. It is, in effect, the most important characteristic that brings people together to take action. It is, the World Bank argues in its Social Capital Initiative (Grootaert and van Bastelaer, 2002), "the glue that binds people who may otherwise not have much in common in terms of geography, wealth, power, leadership, degree of organisation, social cohesion, ethnicity, income, gender, or education." In the realization of shared interest and common goals, it is argued, social capital enables local people to play an active role in their own development (Chambers, 1997).

Several researchers (Campbell and her colleagues at the LSE, for example) have established that the expectations of most community development researchers *vis-à-vis* social capital are unrealistic because the presumed commonality of interest or cooperative culture does not exist in the context of diverse social divisions. It is often argued that such relations of trust, norms of reciprocity and sense of community imply, and require, a relative equality not only of social conditions but of social relations as well as the construction of horizontal networks.

Durston (1999) for one argues (on the basis of his review of research into social capital construction among 5000 or so families and groups of peasants in Guatemala) — and drawing on the wisdom of the anthropologist Mauss — that, as Bourdieu also argued, social capital can indeed be constructed in the context of hierarchical social and political relations. Thus, the "relatively individualistic culture of dependence and domination" displayed by the Chiquimula and Zacapa peasants (embodied in clientelistic and other vertical relations of reciprocity and exchange) coexist with relations of trust and norms of reciprocity, which Durston (1999: 110), after Wilson, argues are "found in all peasant societies everywhere." Durston also argues that, whether constituted as a local community or not, peasants can, and should, build on their cooperative culture by "scaling up" their social capital from small local communities to the leadership at the regional (and even national) level.

Thus Durston, unlike most researchers in this field, does not see the existence of structured social inequalities and unequal relations of political power as an impediment to the construction of social capital. Durston (1999: 115) argues that local communities and organizations of peasants should not only "scale up" their social capital but they should take advantage of the "windows of opportunity" available to them within the existing power structure. He hypothesizes (no argument with evidence presented) that changes in national elites produce "windows of opportunity" for the *emergence* of local social capital and that "alliances with reformist sectors in government open the way to social capital *building*."

Other researchers, less committed to or more critical of the social capital concept, have drawn very different conclusions and "lessons for social-capital building." Campbell and her colleagues, for example, address the tendency of most studies within the field of social capital to counterpose social capital and socioeconomic status (class) as competing explanatory variables. They take this approach to be problematic in the extreme. In fact, they argue, it makes no sense to conceive of social capital (and existing inequalities in its distribution) independently of property in the means of production, material wealth or need deprivation (poverty). If capital is anything it is both part of the problem (poverty reflects the absence or weakness of social capital) and part of the solution (poverty relief requires the accumulation of social capital or collective self-help). But in this regard Bourdieu's analysis of social capital as a means of reproducing social hierarchies (as opposed to the construction of horizontal networks) would be more useful. In this connection Campbell and her colleagues on the Gender Institute's research program on ethnicity, social capital and health inequalities depart from what they regard as the realistic (empirically proven) assumption that material deprivation, socioeconomic status and class, as well as ethnic affiliation, are important sources of existing social inequalities and the variable conditions of social exclusion. Within this context (class and/or ethnic division, and thus the lack of community), it is clear that the fundamental determinants of people's "class situation," to quote Weber rather than Marx, is lack of access to the community's (or society's) economic resources or "assets," such as land, capital and technology. Furthermore, whatever social capital might be, it is distributed unequally and access to it is also structurally (and politically) determined. As Bourdieu argued, and as determined by, among others, Campbell and her associates at the LSE, social (and cultural) forms of capital are more likely to reproduce existing social inequalities than reduce them. Thus, for example, the solution to the problem of poverty posed by the development agencies requires much more than the building, and mobilization, of social capital. Indeed, the only solution provided by social capital seems to be a sense of participation in project-level decision-making, which, as Chhotray (2004) notes, is more illusory than real, allowing the poor only to participate in decisions as to how to spend the meagre poverty-alleviation funds that might come their way. The empowerment of the poor (and, of course, of women and ethnic communities) is more psychological than political; as for politics it is more a negation than an affirmation of their capacity to participate.

Within the framework of the social capital paradigm, development agencies and practitioners define this negation of politics and self-affirmation as "empowerment." But it is clear that empowerment changes nothing; or rather, the "transformative change" of which social capital advocates write relates to the individual, not the system. It implies changing how people view themselves rather than the structure in which are enmeshed. In theory such change is liberating and empowering in that it predisposes and capacitates individuals to rely on their own resources and act collectively to bring about change in their own lives rather than to rely on outside agents or resources. However, the power of the rich, which in its economic and political forms is based on access to and control over financial, physical and natural forms of capital remains intact, untouched by pressures to share or surrender a part of it. The institutions controlled by the rich and powerful remain in place, functioning in their interest. And the policies that determine the overall structure of social and economic conditions also remain in place, free from the pressures for social change exerted by social movements. In the context of local development ("sustainable human development," in its latest formulation) and the new social capital paradigm, the social and political forces of resistance and social change accumulated by these movements are demobilized.

Social Capital, Poverty and Development

According to CEPAL (2003) and the International Fund for Agricultural Investment (IFAD, 2002), at least 44 percent of the population (over 60 percent in the rural sector) in Latin America and the Caribbean live below the conservatively defined poverty line (less than $2 a day). And, over the last two decades, the number of poor people, particularly in rural areas, has increased in both absolute and relative terms — a problem that IFAD (2002) attributes to various structural problems, which, it turns out, have been exacerbated by the free market policies pursued over the past two decades and promoted by the World Bank with repeated almost mantra-like reference to what Williamson (1990) has termed the Washington Consensus.[1]

There is no consensus as to the source of the problem although most institutionally sponsored studies of poverty point towards widespread forms of social exclusion linked to gender and ethnicity (rather than class, which is unaccountably absent).[2] A clear, almost paradigmatic, example of this non-structural and non-political approach towards the problem of poverty can be found in several studies commissioned by the Inter-American Development Bank (IDB) and published in *Who's In and Who's Out: A Study of Social Exclusion in Latin America* (Behrman et al., 2003). Social exclusion, in these and other studies of poverty, is largely a matter of failure to access economic resources and public services such as education, health and housing that address the population's basic needs. As for the difficulties experienced by the poor to gain equitable access to political and economic resources (land, capital, technology, employment, political participation), IFAD, like the authors of the BID publication and other development agencies, turns towards "social values [whose?] and poorly developed rural organizations" (IFAD, 2002). The poor themselves are to blame, the culprits in the problem. And the system long held responsible for the production and reproduction of poverty in its socioeconomic, structural and psychological conditions disappears from analysis — and from the poverty-fighting strategies of the development agencies.

There is also no consensus on the link between macroeconomic policy and growth, and poverty. Not only has the debate on this issue not been brought to any resolution, it continues to rage. But there has emerged a virtual consensus as to how best to confront the problem and proceed — how to wage the war on poverty declared by the World Bank as far back as 1973 (and periodically reaffirmed as the Bank's *raison d'être*) and now joined by a broad coalition of development agencies and governments with a commitment to both macroeconomic policies and reforms that promote both globalization[3] and self-help based on the build-up and mobilization of social capital. The degree of consensus on this strategy for reducing poverty, particularly in regards to social capital, is quite extraordinary.

The multitude of studies commissioned by the World Bank and the other poverty-fighting institutions that comprise the coalition of the committed all seek to establish the dynamics of "good practice." And all of these studies locate good practice in a combination of two factors: building and mobilizing social capital as the critical factor in the development process and a macroeconomic policy regime that provides a supportive institutional framework and facilitating environment.

Conclusion

The concept of social capital was formulated in the context of a paradigmatic shift from a state-led form of development towards a more participatory form. In the 1990s, however, it was reformulated by economists at the World Bank and elsewhere as the central element of a new paradigm for thinking about and bringing about development. The World Bank was the chief instigator of this poverty-oriented approach towards development, the institutional and policy framework for which were given in its structural adjustment program of macroeconomic policy reforms (privatization, deregulation, decentralization, financial and trade liberalization). These policy reforms were defined, and are still presented today as, "pro-poor" — the best, if not the only way out of poverty (World Bank, 2004a).

By the mid-1990s, the notion of social capital as an essential ingredient of development and a large part of the solution to the problem of poverty was given a systematic if ambiguous formulation and was presented at diverse conferences and workshops that brought together "social capital leaders." In this institutional context, social capital was presented as "a person's or group's concern, caring, regard, respect, or sense of obligation for the well-being of another person or group that may produce a potential benefit, advantage, and preferential treatment for another person or group beyond that which might be expected in an [economic] exchange relationship" (Robinson and Siles, n.d.). Within the framework of this concept, social capital is seen to reside in sympathetic relationships of caring, trust, regard and respect. So conceived it was presented as "an essential resource because it contributes to our economic as well as our socio-emotional well-being."

The directors of the SCI (Social Capital Initiative) see social capital as contributing to "our [sic] economic well-being" because it "alters the terms and levels of trade which in turn influence the distribution of incomes." The reason given for social capital to alter the terms and levels of trade is that those who are the objects of another person's caring, trust, regard and respect have the potential to receive preferential treatment. Siles and Robison, co-directors of the SCI, note that this preferential treatment can be demonstrated in recent data on the farmland market, in which land sold to friends and family was discounted by nearly 8 percent — an important improvement and major transformative change? In addition, they argue, social capital "makes important contributions to our [sic] socio-emotional well-being because it supplies socio-emotional goods that meet some of our basic socio-emotional needs, including the need for validation, experiences of caring, and information."

This perspective on social capital reflects a broad consensus view and is representative of the scholarly literature on its "contributions." However, the nature and scope of these contributions to "our well-being" hardly warrant the wildly enthusiastic interest generated by the notion of social capital in the most diverse intellectual and policy-making circles on the left as well as the centre-right of the political spectrum. To understand this we have to turn towards the perceived contributions of social capital in the area of economic and political development. Here social capital is viewed by some as a panacea and by others as a major repository of resources that can be effectively mobilized in the improvement of socioeconomic and political conditions. This improvement relates to issues ranging from poverty and community development to ways of making democracy work. However, the perceived contributions do not explain the enthusiastic interest of so many scholars and practitioners in the notion of social capital. It certainly does not explain at all the dynamics of national and global development. But what it does in its negation of politics is provide a reformist alternative to pressures for more radical social change, for substantive improvement in socioeconomic conditions.

The emergent social capital paradigm aims to be a kind of unified theory, incorporating diverse concepts such as reciprocity, social networks, democratic governance, the strengthening of civil society and the dynamics of participatory development based on resources that the poor have in abundance. The importance of participation in development programming and project design, as in both reformist and radical politics, has been well established as a fundamental principle, a matter not only of (social) equity but of (technical) efficiency. Social capital in this regard is widely seen as highly functional — a useful means of advancing participatory development beyond consultation with the intended beneficiaries to fully engaging them in the development process from the outset (in the words of Chambers and Cernea, "putting the last first" or "the people first"). However, the social capital concept raises the same questions that have surrounded popular participation: is it possible to achieve genuine participation and to bring about required structural changes through an emphasis on consensus and technical targets while negating the politics of development and ignoring patterns of local (and national) power and domination?

This is the problem. In effect, social capital is a means of promoting development without social change — of bringing about improvements in people's lives without affecting existing property relations in the means of social production and the distribution of assets and incomes based on the structure of these relations. In effect, it means empowerment of the poor, providing them with a sense of participation and the opportunity to own their own development efforts, without disempowering the rich. In fact, it would seem, this is what explains both the widespread interest in the social capital concept and the lack of progress in over three decades of fighting poverty by the World Bank and other development organizations and agencies.

Notes

1. The debate as to whether these structural reform policies are pro-growth and pro-poor, as argued by the World Bank or economically as well as socially dysfunctional, as argued by many critics, is not yet settled. See Morley (1995) and Mosley (1999) on the empirical and policy dimensions of the debate within the World Bank and IMF. More recently, Lopez (2004) synthesizes the current state of World Bank knowledge on the relationship between growth, poverty and inequality. The IMF and the World Bank argue that much of the growth that has occurred over the past two decades is to a large extent thanks to these policies and that economic performance would have been less were it not for them. Critics argue the contrary, pointing out that the Bank and Fund's own evidence, and repeated studies, show no systematic correlation between these policies and economic growth, and argue that when there is a correlation it tends to be negative (Mokhiber and Weissman, 2001). In a brief on "corporate globalization and the poor" Mokhiber and Weissman (2001) report on a study by the Center for Economic and Policy Research (CEPR), in which 72% of 89 countries in their survey experienced a decline in their per capita income of at least five percentage points from 1960–1980, a period governed by state-led development, to 1980–2000, an era dominated by the "new economic model" of free market capitalism.

2. Molyneux (2002: 177) for one has noted, and problematized, the fact that women are often central to the forms of social capital that development agencies and governments are all too keen to mobilize in their poverty-relief and community-development programs. In Latin America, not only women but indigenous communities are favourite "targets" of plans and programs for poverty-relief or reduction based on the accumulation of social capital (see, for example, World Bank, 2001).

3. The World Bank has experienced difficulties in maintaining this consensus, and there have been diverse pressures — even from within (for example, Stiglitz, 2002) — to move beyond the consensus and to redesign the reform program: to give it a social dimension (a new social policy) and to provide the entire process a more human face. Nevertheless, a consensus remains as to the basic relevance of the new economic model and the need to stay the course of structural reform, indeed to extend and deepen it. On this, see Kuczynski and Williamson (2003).

Chapter 4

Bad Government, Good Governance

No term has achieved such wide currency as "globalization" in describing the epoch-defining changes that have characterized the past two decades and in prescribing policies of privatization, liberalization and deregulation. Globalization is associated with neoliberal policies designed to create a worldwide capitalist economy. But the promoters and guardians of this new world order have not had an easy time of it. For one thing, the social inequalities generated in the process (see Chapter 2) have not only spawned discontent and social conflict, but the resulting resistance against global capitalist development has been directed against the system, undermining and weakening governments and regimes committed to policies of adjustment and globalization. Under these conditions the guardians of the new neoliberal world order have had to confront a serious political issue of ungovernability (Bardhan, 1997; Kaufmann, Kraay and Zoido-Lobatón, 1999; World Bank, 1994).[1]

"Governance" is a matter of transferring the mechanisms of political control hitherto associated with the state to "civil society." Within the neoliberal model, the state is seen in two ways. On the one hand, it is viewed as Adam Smith did: as predatory and, in the language of the new political economy, susceptible to rentierism and corruption. On the other hand, neoliberals see the state (the government, to be more precise) as an inefficient means of allocating society's productive resources. Within the parameters of the old and now defunct economic model in place since the 1950s, the government, in its policies of strategic nationalization, protectionism and market regulations distorted the normal working of the market, leading to a withdrawal of capital from the production process and generating thereby widespread problems of poverty and unemployment as well as fiscal imbalance. Within these neoliberal optics, the state required institutional and policy reform in the direction of macroeconomic equilibrium (balanced budgets/accounts), structural adjustment and administrative decentralization — to surrender thereby its capacity for resource allocation and reduce its economic role *vis-à-vis* responsibilities for development and social programming. The political dimension to these reforms involved democratization, not so much in a return to the rule of law and electoral politics as a change in the relation of the state to civil society. This, I argue, is the crux of the governability/governance issue.

The problem — for the promoters of globalization — is that neoliberalism is economically dysfunctional, profoundly exclusionary in social terms and politically unsustainable, generating as it does destabilizing forces of resistance and opposition. It is precisely as a means of dealing with this problem that the international organizations of development and finance have turned so decisively towards democratization and the strengthening of civil society, contracting nonprofit voluntary associations (NGOs) and converting them into "strategic partners." The agenda here is to enlist the help of these organizations in defusing the fire of revolutionary ferment in the countryside — to provide the rural poor and the popular sector of society with an alternative to social movements and their confrontational politics.

This chapter explores the political dynamics of this process, which involves social movements, formed as means of resisting the neoliberal agenda of globalization and free market development, being beset by forces designed to demobilize them, to divert the struggle for state power in one or more directions towards electoral politics, reformist social organizations or local development.

Civil Society, Development and Democracy

Globalization is one of several ideas advanced in the lexicon of the new global economy. The marketing of globalization as a policy of deregulation, liberalization and privatization was accompanied by the resurrection of a term, "civil society," used by the rationalist humanists of the eighteenth century Enlightenment to distinguish a sphere independent from the state. In the context of a neoconservative attack on the welfare/developmental state, the idea of civil society achieved prominence in political and developmental discourse, particularly in connection to successive waves of democratization, beginning in Latin America and Eastern Europe and spreading across the developing world. Civil society was seen as an agent for limiting authoritarian government, minimizing the socially atomizing and unsettling effects of market forces, enforcing political accountability and improving governance. Reconsideration of the limits of state action also led to an increased awareness of the potential role of civic organizations in the provision of public goods and social services, either separately or in some kind of synergistic relationship with state institutions. The idea of civil society, like that of globalization, was converted into a discursive weapon and an ideological tool in the service of advancing the neoliberal agenda.

Academic discourse on civil society, however, has moved beyond this agenda and can now be put into three ideological categories — conservative, liberal and radical. Liberals generally see civil society as a countervailing force against an unresponsive and corrupt state and exploitative corporations that disregard environmental issues and human rights abuses (Kamat, 2003).

Conservatives, on the other hand, see in civil society the beneficial effects of globalization for the development of democracy and economic progress — for advancing the idea of freedom in its historic march against its enemies (Chan, 2001). As for those scholars who share a belief in the need for radical change, civil society is seen as a repository of the forces of resistance and opposition, forces than can be mobilized into a counter-hegemonic bloc or a global anti-globalization movement.

In effect, academic discourse in its diverse ideological currents converges in its support of civil society, viewing it as an agent for change in one form or the other. The strengthening of civil society (nongovernmental, social and civic organizations) in the 1980s and 1990s is offered as proof of its capacity for autonomous development and the virtues of democracy. In this process of democratic renewal (or "re-democratization," as it is referred to in the literature), NGOs are assigned a predominant role as front-line agents of a participatory and democratic form of development and politics, to convince the rural poor thereby of the virtues of community-based local development and the need to reject the confrontational politics of the social movements.

In the 1980s there was an explosion of NGOs, many of which were formed in the wake of a retreating state. It is estimated that the vast majority of the 37,000 or so NGOs operating today in developing countries were formed in the 1980s or the 1990s. As noted above, NGOs were contracted by international organizations — and the governments engaged in the international development project — to spread the gospel of the free market and democracy — and to speak for the virtues of social-democratic, civic organization and action within the local spaces available within the national power structure. Despite the serious reservations of many governments in the developing world, NGOs were viewed as vastly preferable to the social movements, which were generally oriented towards collective action against the power structure, seeking to change this structure rather than seeking some accommodation within it. In this political context, NGOs are enlisted by overseas development agencies and governments as partners in the process of "sustainable human development" and "good governance" — as watchdogs of state deviancy, to ensure state transparency (inhibit or prevent corruption and rentierism) and as participants in the formulation of public policy. The institutional framework for this participatory form of development and politics (and governance rather than government) would be established by the decentralization of decision-making capacity and associated responsibilities from the national to the local level and by the institution of good governance, that is, a democratic regime in which the responsibility for human security and political order is not restricted to the government and other institutions of the state but is widely shared by different civil society organizations (BID, 1996, 2000; OECD, 1997; UNDP, 1996; World Bank, 1994).

The global phenomenon and explosive growth of NGOs reflects a new policy and political consensus that they are *de facto*, and by design, effective agents for democratic change, an important means for instituting an alternative form of development that is initiated from below, socially inclusive, equitable, participatory and sustainable. This consensus view is reinforced by evidence that the NGO channel of overseas development assistance (ODA) is by and large dedicated to political rather than economic development — to ensure transparency, promote democracy in the process of change, inculcate relevant values and respect for democratic norms of behaviour and encourage the adoption of civil politics (dialogue, consultations, negotiation) rather than the confrontationalist politics of the social movements.

The leading role of civil society organizations (CSOs) in this regard (political development) foretells a reworking of "democracy" in ways that coalesce with global capitalism and the neoliberal agenda. Indeed, a well placed development practitioner in the U.K. (Wallace, 2003) has wondered aloud (and put in print) whether NGOs have been used by the international organizations as their Trojan horse — and, not to put too fine a point on it, as agents of global neoliberalism. Global policy forums and institutions, such as the OECD's Development Centre, USAID, the World Bank and the Inter-American Development Bank, as well as the U.N.'s operational agencies such as the UNDP, have all turned towards the NGOs as "forces of democratization" in the "economic reform process" (Kamat, 2003: 65). In this, Ottaway (2003: vi) argues, they function as agents of "democratic promotion," a "new activity in which the aid agencies and NGOs [originally] embarked [upon] with some trepidation and misgivings" but that in the early 1990s "came of age."

Civil Society and the State

In the 1990s, the perception of NGOs as "Trojan horses for global neoliberalism" (Wallace, 2003) also came of age. But the effectiveness of NGOs in this regard is not without controversy. Indeed, it has occasioned somewhat of a debate between liberals, in general favourably disposed towards the NGOs, and conservatives, who view them as "false saviours of international development" (Kamat, 2003). Radical political economists tend to view NGOs as instruments, either knowingly or oftentimes unwittingly, of outside interests. And, in the same context, both economic development and democracy appear as masks for an otherwise hidden agenda — to impose the policy and institutional framework of the new world order against resistance.

This apparent convergence between the left and the right in a critical assessment of NGOs points towards several problems involved in the use of the state as an instrument of political power. From a liberal reformist perspective, the state needs to be strengthened but it also needs to be democratized

71

in the service of a more inclusive and participatory approach towards policy design and implementation. From a neoliberal (and politically conservative) perspective, however, the state is *the* problem. On the one hand, it is an inefficient means of allocating the productive resources of the system. On the other, as Adam Smith argued, it is a predatory device with a tendency to serve special interests and to capture rents from state-sponsored and regulated economic activities. State officials, it is added by contemporary advocates of this view, such as the economists at the World Bank, are subject to pressures that more often than not result in their corruption. The solution: a minimalist state, subject to the democratizing pressures of civil society, i.e., groups and organizations able to secure the transparency of the policy-making process.

And what of the state as viewed from the lens of an alternative, more radical political economy? The state appears as an instrument of class rule, a repository of concentrated political power needed to turn the process of national development around — in a socialist direction. The essence of what is now widely regarded as the politics of the old left — or the old politics of the left — is a struggle over state power. Both leftist political parties and the social movements tend to be oriented in this direction, albeit in a new political context, which has seen the emergence of a new perspective and way of doing politics — the politics of "no-power," which is to avoid confrontations with the structures of political and economic power and instead build on the social capital of the poor.

In the academic world, the politics of state power is theoretically constructed in these ways. But what about the real world? With specific reference to developments in Latin America, the main pattern of political development over the past two decades seems to have been a twofold devolution/involution of state power. On the one hand, the policy and institutional framework for political decision-making has been subjected to what has been termed the Washington Consensus, with a corresponding shift of political power (*vis-à-vis* macroeconomic policy) towards Washington-based "international" institutions such as the World Bank and the IMF. On the other hand, a democratic "reform" process has resulted in the institution of the "rule of law" and the decentralization of government to the local, as well as the strengthening of civil society.

The latter development is based on partnerships between international organizations and governments on the one hand, and civil society on the other. And it is not happenstance; it is based on a conscious strategy pursued by the major representative organizations of global capital and the new world economic order. Among these organizations can be found the World Bank, the regional banks like the IDB, overseas development agencies such as USAID, the Development Centre of the OECD and operational agencies of the U.N.

72

system, such as the UNDP, United Nations Environment Program (UNEP), Food and Agriculture Organization (FAO) and World Health Organization (WHO). Each of these organizations pursues a partnership strategy with NGOs and other civil society organizations, setting up a division (or "office") to work with them, officially registering those prepared to work with them in a common agenda of democratic development, poverty alleviation and environmental protection — an alternative form of participatory, socially inclusive and human (economic and social) development.

Much of the current academic discourse on the role of NGOs in the economic and political development process focuses on the issue of improving their organizational effectiveness as well as their accountability — and their autonomy *vis-à-vis* governments and the donor organizations. Several umbrella organizations within the NGO sector have sought assiduously to ensure greater independence from both donors and the governments that hire private voluntary organizations (PVOs) to execute their projects and programs. But generally speaking, these efforts have not met with any success. More often than not, as in the case of the U.S., the major NGOs have not only met with resistance on the part of the donor community but outright efforts to bring NGOs into line. In 2003, the director of USAID bluntly informed an assembly of NGOs brought together by Interaction, an umbrella organization of American NGOs, that they would have to do a better job of acknowledging their ties to government, as private contractors of public policy, or risk losing funding. My own research indicates that a substantial number of NGOs in recent years have become increasingly dependent on this funding.

Some go so far as to argue that the presumed role of the NGO is a mirage that obscures the workings and interests of a powerful state (imperialism), national elites and the predations of private capital. Hayden (2002) argues this from a conservative perspective. However, I argue the same point from a more radical perspective on NGOs as agents of imperialism, private contractors of governments in the North, particularly the U.S. Governments in the South, in many cases, are only reluctantly and belatedly moving away from a somewhat sceptical, if not hostile, attitude — born of experiences with NGOs as watchdogs of the state, particularly in terms of any propensities towards authoritarianism and corruption, from the perspective of an agenda to promote democracy in its relation to civil society. In a situation of widespread authoritarianism, violation of human rights and other abuses of political power, the NGOs throughout the 1980s had no fundamental problem in assuming their intermediary role in the front line of economic and political development. However, in the changed, more democratic context of the 1990s, many NGOs began to experience serious concerns that, in effect (by design if not intent), they were advancing the agenda of the donors rather than that of the urban and rural poor, many of whom were not oriented towards alternative development and representative democracy but rather toward more substantive social change based on direct action and social movements, that is, popular democracy. The major NGOs redoubled their efforts to secure greater autonomy from donors, to be able to thereby respond better to the concerns and priorities of the popular movement. As a result, they tend to find themselves caught between a widespread concern to increase their independence from their sponsors and the efforts of these sponsoring organizations to incorporate them into the development and political process as strategic partners in a common agenda.

NGOs and the New Policy Agenda

In the 1980s, development agencies such as USAID were fundamentally concerned to use PVOs to mediate between themselves and grassroots communities in the delivery of ODA and, at the same time to promote democracy both in the relation of the state to civil society and in the politics of grassroots organizations — good governance, in the official parlance (Annan, 1998; BID, 1996; Blair, 1997; Kaufman et al., 1999; Mitlin, 1998; OECD, 1997; UNDP, 1996).

In the late 1980s and early 1990s, however, there occurred a marked shift in practice, signalled with a change in discourse — from a third sector discourse, privileging NGOs, to a civil society discourse, which was more inclusive, particularly as regards profit-making enterprises and business associations that make up the private sector. This shift in discourse coincided with a widespread recognition in official circles of the need to reform the structural adjustment program — to give it a social dimension and a human face (Cornia, Jolly and Stewart, 1987; Salop, 1992).

Political discourse in the 1980s reflected the political dynamics of an ideological shift from a state-led development process to a market-led form of development based on the privatization of public enterprise. A third sector discourse represented a concern for an alternative, more participatory form of development and politics predicated on neither the agency of the state (from above) nor the workings of the market (from the outside) but initiated within civil society (from below). From the perspective of the overseas development agencies, the IFIs and governments, however, this new discourse was problematic. For one thing, it was directed against both the market and the state — against public *and* private enterprise. For another, it worked against efforts of the overseas development agencies to incorporate the private sector into the development process. The problem was twofold. One was how to overcome widespread antipathy towards profit-making, private enterprises — to see them as part of a possible solution rather than as a major problem. Another was to convince the private sector that profits can be made in the process of social development.

74

The second problem remains a concern even into the twenty-first century, causing difficulties for the U.N. in its efforts to establish its "global compact" with the private sector (UNDP, 1998). Regarding the first problem, a civil society discourse has proven to be both useful and effective. It has indeed allowed the overseas development agencies to incorporate the private sector into the development project as a strategic partner in the process of economic growth and "sustainable human development." The perceived need for this was established by evaluation studies suggesting that NGOs provided a useful channel for ODA in regard to political development (promotion of democracy) and capacity-building/strengthening (social capital) but an inefficient means of activating production and employment and providing financial services. The conclusion was drawn that what was needed was a new strategy, based on the agency of local governments working in partnership with overseas development agencies and NGOs.

Matters of Good Governance and Alternative Development

The evolution of community-based organizations (CBOs) or grassroots organizations (GROs) within civil society illustrates the changed environment in which NGOs now operate. For Kamat (2003: 65), it also points towards "grave implications" of the new scenario for "development, democracy and political stability." CBOs are locally based organizations that champion a "bottom up" or people-centred approach towards development. They are, Kamat points out, particularly vulnerable to what he views as "unexpected patronage" of the donor agencies. What is most surprising is that Kamat sees this patronage as unexpected. Community-based or grassroots development organizations emerged in the post–Second World War period in response to the failure of developmentalist states to ensure the basic needs of the poor — in the 1970s *the* declared development agenda of the overseas development agencies and associated governments in the North. As well as a foreign policy concern with the spread of communism and the perceived impulse of some popular organizations and governments to take the road of social revolution towards development, USAID set up, sponsored and financed a number of PVOs to act as private contractors of the government's foreign policy agenda. A large number of community-based organizations in Latin America were similarly financed and sponsored.

In many cases the leaders of these CBOs had been active in women's or radical left movements and had become disillusioned with the politics of what would later be referred to as the "old left." These CBOs generally favoured a social rather than political approach towards development, with a concern for social justice and local issues. In this relatively apolitical context these CBOs were aggressively courted by both northern NGOs and overseas development agencies such as the World Bank, which, to some extent, preferred to finance and support these local organizations directly rather than work through the northern NGOs. More often than not, these CBOs accepted the financial support, if not tutelage, of the agency as a necessary evil and by times even as a virtue (building the capacity for self-help and social capital).

The nature of their work requires CBOs (or "intermediary grassroots organizations," in the World Bank's language) to interact directly with local communities on a daily basis, building relationships of cooperation designed to understand local needs and tailor projects to these needs. The work of such social activists and organizations — identified by Rains Kothari as "non-party political formations" — often was and sometimes still is looked upon suspiciously by governments in Latin America, many of which, according to Ottaway (2003), are democratic in form but not in content (semi-authoritarian) and the targets of democratization efforts. In the interest of strengthening civil society, the overseas development agencies increasingly have turned towards these CBOs rather than the northern NGOs as their executing agents. The dominant strategy, however, is based on partnership with local governments, civil society organizations (CSOs) and the private sector — an approach facilitated by widespread implementation of a decentralization policy (Rondinelli, McCullough and Johnson, 1989).

The history of the community development movement in the 1950s and 1960s signified the emergence of a "pluralist democratic culture" in many developing countries as well as a concern for local development within the framework of liberal reforms of national policy. But the dominant trend was for economic and political development based on the agency of the central government. However, in the new policy environment of structural, free market reform, this incipient democratic culture was cultivated by the return of civilian constitutional rule and, at another level, by widespread policies of privatization and decentralization. With the retreat of the state from the economy and its social and developmental responsibilities, it was left to civil society to pick up the slack — in the form of emergent, self-help organizations of the urban poor and a myriad of community-based and nongovernmental organizations, which had to deal with issues of social and economic development such as health, housing, food kitchens (*comedores*, or communal dining halls), capacity building and self-employment. The formation of this civil society was a prominent feature of the 1980s.

In the environment created by the new economic model of neoliberal free market capitalist development, CBOs became a useful, even essential, adjunct of the policies pursued by the donor agencies such as USAID — polices designed to promote a "capacity for self-help." The failure of a state-led model of economic development, combined with conditions of a fiscal crisis, weakened state infrastructure and a decline in state entitlements to the poor, led the donor agencies to channel an even greater share of foreign aid through CBOs and a proliferating number of NGOs. In this connection, Gore, on the vice-presidential campaign trail in 1994, stated that within five years up to 50 percent of USAID would be so channelled. Similarly, it was reported that the U.K. was increasingly inclined to fund locally based NGOs (i.e., CBOs) directly, bypassing its own NGOs such as Oxfam.

The conjunction of a retreating minimalist state and the exponential increase in community-based NGOs led to the conclusion that the phenomenon was analogous to "the franchising of the state" Kamat, 2003: 66). The donor agencies and the IFIs recommended the privatization of both economic activity and social services — a trend that in any case was already underway — and the allocation of ODA to community-based NGOs for the same programs. Under these conditions the "grassroots" NGOs proliferated, as did the northern NGOs, anxious to occupy the spaces left by a retreating state.

From the Global to the Local

The influx of external funds, combined with pressure to step into the spaces vacated by the state, forced many NGOs, particularly those that were community-based, to restructure their activities in line with the new partnership approach of the overseas development agencies. In the process, according to Kamat (2003: 66), the organizational ethic that distinguished CBOs as democratic and representative of the popular will is being slowly undermined. First of all, CBOs generally have an active membership base within the communities in which they work, be they urban slum dwellers or poor peasant farmers. However, these target or client groups are themselves increasingly involved in efforts to strengthen civil society, i.e., they are incorporated into decision-making processes at the local level. This form of direct or popular democracy both enthralls the donor agencies and the left but it also inconveniences the former and embarrasses the latter. On the one hand, it identifies the unique strength of NGOs, which, according to the World Bank, consists of "their ability to reach poor communities and remote areas, promote local participation, and operate at a low cost, identify local needs [and] build on local resources." On the other hand, direct democracy is inconvenient because of "its limited replicability, self-sustainability, managerial... capacity, narrow context for programmes and politicization" (Kamat, 2003: 66).

NGOs were slowly but surely transformed from organizations set up to serve the poor into what the World Bank describes as "operational NGOs" — private contractors of World Bank policies that operate within "poor constituencies" with a more or less apolitical and managerial approach (micro-project), but not rooted in or part of these communities. First of all, implementation of local projects calls for training in specific skills rather than a more general education that might involve an analysis of social and economic policies and processes. As a result, NGO after NGO has been forced to adopt a more narrowly economic and apolitical approach to working with the poor than had often been the case. At the same time, local participation in decision-making becomes limited to small-scale projects that draw on local resources with the injection of minimal external funds for poverty alleviation, which are not predicated on substantial social change in the distribution of, and access to, local and national resources. Local community groups are left to celebrate their empowerment (decision-making capacity *vis-à-vis* the distribution of local resources and the allocation of any poverty-alleviation funds), while the powers-that-be retain their existing (and disproportionate) share of national and local resources — and the legal entitlement to their property — without the pressure for radical change. In effect, the forced professionalization of the community-based NGOs and their subsequent depoliticization represent two sides of the same development, producing a common set of effects: to keep the existing power structure intact while promoting a degree (and a local form) of change and development.

Decentralization and Participation: Empowerment or Depoliticization?

According to ECLAC (1990) in its well-known programmatic statement of its alternative to the neoliberal model, "participation" is the "missing link" between the process of "productive transformation" (technological conversion of the production apparatus) and "equity" (expansion of the social basis of this apparatus). The World Bank had recently discovered that participation is a matter not only of equity, as ECLAC understood it, but of economic efficiency. This recognition, stated as early as 1989, did not lead the Bank to adopt a more inclusive approach to macroeconomic policy, which, by all accounts, was profoundly exclusive, designed to benefit only those free enterprises that were both productive and competitive. In fact, this was the first pillar of any and all alternative models of economic and social development supported by the Bank.

In any case, the World Bank is in essential agreement with all of the other operational agencies of the U.N. system that the decentralization of government is an indispensable condition for both a more democratic and participatory form of economic and social (that is, *integral* or *human*) development and for establishing a regime of "good governance" — political order on the basis of as little government as possible but rather with what amounts to a system of social control based on consensus within civil society, at least among what the World Bank and IDB define as the "stakeholders." On this basis, the Bank, like the IDB, has been a major advocate of the policies of decentralization as well as the virtues of local democracy and local development (OECD, 1997; Rondinelli, McCullough and Johnson, 1989; World Bank, 1994).

The new emphasis on project implementation at the local level provided by widespread implementation of administrative (and betimes financial) decentralization has drawn attention away from the need for large-scale structural change in the allocation/distribution of society's productive resources. Development projects are implemented within available, limited local spaces. The programmatic focus on individual capacities minimizes the concern for the structural (social and political) causes of poverty and rejects efforts to deal with them in a confrontational matter. This promotes instead pacific (democratic) forms of political action — consultation, dialogue, negotiations, etc.

This apolitical and managerial (micro-project) approach to community development draws on the liberal notion of empowerment, in which the poor are encouraged to find an entrepreneurial solution to their problems. The OECD (1997) defines its approach in terms of "helping people of the world develop their skills and abilities *to solve their own problems*" (my emphasis). As noted above (and see Bebbington et al., 2006), the World Bank adopted a strategy of empowerment and participation — at least at the level of rhetoric (without any effective or specific mechanisms for bringing about these conditions) in the interest not only of equity but economic efficiency.

This entrepreneurial or neoliberal notion of empowerment is altogether different from the critical understanding of it as a form of alternative development promoted by CBOs. In this neoliberal discourse on empowerment the individual, as a repository of human resources (knowledge, skills, capacities to decide and act), is posited as both the problem and the solution to the problem of poverty. Of course, this is congruent with the utilitarian notion of the individual, when freed from government constraints imposed by the state, as an agent of rational choice (to maximize gain and minimize or avoid losses), diverting attention away from the issue of the state's responsibility to redistribute market-generated incomes and the perceived need for radical change not in the direction of the market but away from it.

The "growth with equity" (redistributive growth/basic needs) approach of the liberal reformers in the 1970s was focused on the role of the state as an agency empowered to redistribute market-generated incomes via a policy of progressive taxation, redirecting income to social and development programs designed to benefit not just the poor but the whole population — to meet their basic needs. At the level of the NGOs, this basic needs approach included in fact, if not by design, a policy of conscientization — educating the poor about structural issues such as the concentration of economic and political power in the hands (and institutions) of the elite and their own political rights. In the Latin American context, Acción Católica was particularly oriented this way, on the basis of liberation theology and implemented at the level of extension work in the form of pastorals. However, from the perspective of the donors, this approach was problematic and even politically dangerous in that it could — and in different contexts did — turn the poor to reach beyond institutional and policy reform (and self-help micro-projects) towards more radical forms of change based on collective action, even social revolution.

The issue for the poor was whether they should be empowered as individuals to take decisions related to local self-help development (basically how and where to spend poverty-alleviation funds) or as part of a collective to take direct action against the structure and holders of economic and political power. There is a significant political dimension to this issue: does empowerment of the poor necessarily entail a relative disempowerment of the rich — forcing them to give up some of their property (a share of society's productive resources and associated incomes) and share with the poor their decision-making capacity? The politics of this question was clear enough, establishing for NGOs the role that they would come to play — not the role they would take for themselves but that which they were cast into as private contractors of public policy.

In terms of actual developments from the 1970s, the effect has been not to empower the poor (increase their decision-making control over conditions that directly affected their livelihoods) but rather to depoliticize their organizations, inhibiting the political mobilizing of forces of opposition to the system. Poor communities have been empowered to take decisions regarding how to spend the miserable poverty-alleviation funds that come their way — in exchange for a commitment to accept the existing institutionality and the macroeconomic policies that support it.

Studies in different countries confirm this practice and the role of the NGOs in regard to it. For example, Mirafab (Kamat 2003: 69) traces the conversion of Mexican NGOs from organizations geared towards "deep structural change through consciousness, making demands and opposing the government" into organizations aimed at an "incremental improvement of the poor's living conditions through community self-reliance." This process was not unique to Mexico. Indeed, in cases too numerous to mention, community-based NGOs moved away from empowerment programs that involved the political organization of the poor based on conscientization. Instead, at the behest of the donors, NGOs turned towards a "skills training" approach to the mitigation of poverty by providing social and economic inputs based on a technical assessment of the needs, capacities and assets of the poor.

The dynamics of this process as they relate to the role of the NGOs can be summarized as follows. The World Bank's operational NGOs establish an instrumental relationship with their constituency in the marginal communities of the rural and urban poor, allowing development experts to proceed as if the demands of the people are already known and predefined — demands such as roads, electricity, midday meals, birth control for women, micro-finance and poultry farming, to name but a few. Kamat (2003: 65) notes that empowerment and participation are simulated by NGOs and their donor agencies even as their practices are increasingly removed from the meaning of these terms, which is to say, they are decapacitated or disempowered in regard to bringing about the changes needed to improve their access to society's productive resources.

The popularity of micro-finance projects in the practice of development can be understood in a situation wherein the state is no longer primarily responsible for creating employment, let alone improving the access of the poor to productive resources such as land. In the early 1980s there was a strong push to both privatize the means of production and to deregulate markets, liberating the private sector from government constraint as well as emphasizing its role in regards to economic development. In this climate even the state's responsibilities and funding in the area of social development (education, health and welfare and social security) were cut back, shifting the former to the level of local governments and cutting the latter in the interest of balancing the government's national accounts and budget. Empowerment of the poor, as noted by OECD and echoed by USAID and other donor organizations, is defined as and means self-help — to support GROs in their self-help ventures.

However, rather than assisting the poor in improving their access to productive resources such as land (natural resources), financial capital (credit) or physical capital (technology), the poor are expected to build on their own social capital — to enhance their own capacities *vis-à-vis* livelihood security and sustainability (UNRISD, 2000).

To place these issues in a critical perspective, micro-finance or credit projects, in which risks are shifted to the individual entrepreneurs, often poor women who are forced to compete for limited resources and opportunities in a very restricted market environment, are well-suited to the neoliberal agenda. The promise of livelihood security and local development thus translates into optimal utilization of one's own capacities and resources rather than working against the system. Kamat (2003: 65) concludes that the democratization that NGOs represent is more symbolic than substantive. For the most part they are engaged in producing a particular kind of democracy, one that coincides with a neoliberal economic context. Heloise Weber (2002: 145), research fellow at the University of Warwick's Centre for the Study of Globalisation and Regionalisation, observes that micro-credit, particularly in its Bolivian paradigmatic form, is a strategy initiated *from the outside* (at the level of global institutions) as a means of advancing the globalization agenda — "a tool that facilitates the imperatives of globalization" — and, she adds, a tool used "for its global governance implications."

One of these implications is that

the harmonization of local social policy at the global level... provides for a coherent set of tools that may facilitate as well govern the globalization agenda. The microcredit agenda (and thus, the "poverty alleviation" strategy of the World Bank)... is conducive to facilitating policy changes at the local level according to the logic of globalization... while at the same time advancing its potential to discipline locally in the global governance agenda. (Weber, 2002: 146)

As a policy initiated not at the national (or even local) level but, as Weber notes, at the level of global institutions (the World Bank, etc.), micro-credit or finance is an explicating example of what has been referred to as the "supra-nationalization of local social policy." Micro-credit, based more on the social capital of the poor than an infusion of "social funds" (the most popular means of implementing micro-credit programs), also has "critical implications for political struggle" (Weber, 2002: 146).

Conclusion

The push towards liberal democracy over the past two decades is part of a good governance strategy pursued under the aegis of the World Bank and other overseas development organizations. Other elements of this strategy include (1) democratizing the relation of civil society to the state; (2) strengthening civil society *vis-à-vis* its capacity for participation in the formulation of public policy; and (3) empowerment of the poor via the accumulation of their social capital — building networks in support of a self-help strategy.

The major means for bringing about democratization in this form has been decentralization, a policy instituted by many countries in the 1980s and 1990s. Decentralization has taken diverse forms but most generally involves a delegation of central government responsibilities and policy-making capacity to lower levels of government. Ironically, it was Agusto Pinochet in the early 1970s who pioneered this policy, as well as the package of "sweeping economic reforms" used by the World Bank to construct its neoliberal program of structural adjustment reforms. In regard to this policy of decentralization, Pinochet spoke of "teaching the world a lesson in democracy" — what the Bank (1989, 1994) has come to define as "good governance": rule by consensus engineered via the participation of local communities in decisions relating to conditions that directly affect them. The crux of this policy is popular participation, conceived of by ECLAC (1990) as "the missing link" between the neoliberal concern with productive transformation and the principle of equity promoted by structuralists and reformists. In the 1980s the notion of popular participation was enshrined in the notion of good governance and treated as a fundamental principle both in project design and the delivery of development assistance and government services.

But this concern for good governance is not what it appears to be. Behind this notion is a fundamentally political concern to establish the conditions needed to implement the new economic model of free market capitalist development — to ensure the capacity and the political will of national governments to "stay the course" (structural adjustment, globalization) and thereby to ensure the stability of the new world economic order. And just as important is the operational and political need to subjugate local (national) economies and emerging markets to the dictates of global capital. This is the agenda of U.S. or Euroamerican imperialism. It is this agenda that defines the ideology of globalization and the agency of organizations for international development. Both globalization and development as geo-strategic meta-projects can be unmasked as disguised forms of imperialism, raising serious questions about nongovernmental organizations in the process.

It can be concluded that NGOs play a critically important role in advancing the imperialist agenda. In the 1970s many were converted into frontline development agencies — to spread the gospel of the virtues of social and political reform and, within the context of local development micro-projects, help offset growing pressures for revolutionary change. In the 1980s, in a different context (external debt crisis, implementation of a new economic model, privatization and state reform, democratization), the NGOs once again were enlisted in the World Bank's declared war against poverty as agents of popular democracy and alternative development — as partners in the development enterprise and to promote a nonconfrontational approach towards social change.

This project was advanced and the process consolidated in the 1990s, creating conditions that facilitated the workings of imperialism. A critical factor in this consolidation was the creation of client regimes committed to a neoliberal model of capitalist development and globalization. But just as critical was the incorporation of civil society into the development and democratization process. A part of civil society, in the organizational form of social movements, engaged the political project of opposition to neoliberalism and globalization — mobilizing the resistance against neoliberalism into a popular movement, or (in Gramscian language) a "counter-hegemonic bloc" of popular power. However, another part of civil society has been complicit with imperialism, providing it important support and services. The actual intent of these NGOs is not the issue. In many cases the individuals involved genuinely believe that they are in acting in the interest of the local communities, providing the poor tangible benefits. But we need to look at whose interests are in fact served by their actions as strategic partners of the World Bank and other international organizations. The critical question is how NGOs play into the relationship of the state to the social movements and the struggle for political power?

Note

1. One of the first to recognize and define this problem was Samuel Huntington, who, in 1975, together with two trilateralist colleagues, submitted a report to the Trilateral Commission (Crozier et al., 1975) that identified democracy as a seriously flawed system in its tendency to generate expectations and forces of radical change that are not easily contained within the system. Ten years later Robert Kapstein, Director of the U.S. Council of Foreign Relations, one of Washington's critically important foreign policy forums concerned with the project of constructing a new world order (or in the language of neoconservatism, "the new imperialism"), raised the spectre of political instability and ungovernability in the context of a trend towards excessive social inequalities, growing poverty and the extreme polarization of world society (Kapstein, 1996). The World Bank in particular took this question seriously, seeing it as central to the development enterprise and its mandate — to alleviate poverty, via a less exclusionary process and if necessary by means of improving access of the poor to society's productive resources (World Bank, 1994). The following year, however, ten years after Kapstein's article in *Foreign Affairs*, saw the emergence of a problem that assumed crisis proportions in Asia mid-1997: the Asian Financial Crisis. The problems associated with this crisis put the question of governance on the international agenda as a matter of urgency: to control the vast pools of volatile capital by means of a "new financial architecture" (on this see, inter alia, Stiglitz, 2002). More recently, the issue of governance has been re-examined in the context of a revived concern that the polarization between the poor and the rich in world society and the global economy is threatening to undermine democracy and create political instability (Karl, 2000).

Chapter 5

Dynamics of Market-led Development

This chapter addresses some critical development issues in the context of free market neoliberal capitalism. In this form, development is profoundly exclusionary and uneven, generating widespread conditions of poverty and social discontent — and equally widespread pressures for social change and an alternative form of local development.

The chapter begins with a synopsis of the problems of poverty and social exclusion that affect a large part of the rural population in Latin America and elsewhere in the Third World. It then introduces case studies of rural development practice in Bolivia and Peru before turning to the dynamics of struggle associated with the social movements, which are generally more oriented towards a politics of mass mobilization and revolutionary change than local development.

The chapter concludes with a summary of the alternative paths to social change taken by organizations of the popular movement. The conclusion is that in the current conjuncture there are three basic paths to social change. Two of these, those of electoral politics and social mobilization, are paved with power, which is to say, they are oriented towards control of the state, a critical repository of political power. The third path towards social change is predicated on a non-confrontational, "no-power" approach, which is to seek improvements and change (i.e., development) within the local spaces of the power structure without directly challenging the holders of this power.

The Pillars of Social Exclusion and Rural Poverty

The study of development can be traced back to the immediate post–Second World War period, but the war against global poverty — identifying poverty as the central issue and a sustained effort to redress it, reducing its incidence, eradicating its extreme forms and alleviating its worst conditions — can be traced back to the World Bank under the presidency of Robert McNamara, hitherto Secretary of State for External Affairs, in charge of prosecuting the war on Vietnam. As of that point, some three decades back, the World Bank has periodically affirmed the centrality of poverty on the development agenda, leading the war against it in battlefields across the world.

The war on poverty over the years has been waged though numerous campaigns and in many settings but without, it would appear, any appreciable results. After three decades of diverse development efforts the problem is as entrenched and widespread as ever, affecting, it is conservatively estimated, over 40 percent of the world's population — no less than in 1973 when the problem was first discovered. This raises a number of questions. Why, for example, have these efforts yielded so few results of benefit to the world's poor? Is the problem that intractable? Has the war been misdirected or associated efforts misguided, based on erroneous theoretical models or strategies that fail to identify the critical factors of remedial action?

One reason for the failure of so much apparent effort to bring about social change or development is that the problem is often misconstrued. Academic explanations of the underlying structure that produced and reproduces poverty can be placed into two categories: those that relate to the concept of exploitation (extraction of surplus value from the activities of the direct producer, or worker) and those that focus on conditions of marginalization, or, in more recent parlance, social exclusion (Atal and Yen, 1995; Bessis, 1995). At issue here is whether the conditions of poverty are connected to the workings of the operating economic system (neoliberal capitalism) or whether they reflect a relative lack of participation in this system, i.e., exclusion.

On one point there appears to be a virtual consensus in the academic literature: that the neoliberal model is profoundly exclusionary. Prior to the current era of neoliberal globalization, analysts focused not on this feature but on the exploitative nature of the system and on the social conditions of this exploitation, such as low wages, inequalities in the distribution of income and poverty. But today it is possible to argue that the dominant feature and the greatest social impact of the capitalist development process in its neoliberal form relates not so much to its exploitative character as to its propensity towards social exclusion (Paugam, 1996). The neoliberal model is geared to benefit but a small segment of proprietors and business operators, those few private enterprises — estimated at some 15 percent of the total — that are able to compete in the world market. Another segment of private sector enterprises, estimated at around 35 percent, are deemed to have productive capacity but are oriented predominantly towards the domestic market. Under the neoliberal model these enterprises are subjected to the forces of the free market, with little support from government policies, leading to a process of economic restructuring that, in theory, shakes out the most inefficient. By a number of accounts, at least half of all enterprises — primarily those based on the peasant economy in the rural sector and, in the urban environment, micro-enterprises in the informal sector — are left to twist in the winds of change.

The neoliberal capitalist development process has resulted in a growing mass of producers and workers separated from their means of production and excluded from both the political and economic processes of this development. Under these conditions of social exclusion, a large and expanding part of Latin America's rural population is experiencing a social crisis of devastating proportions (Ghai, 1991; Paugam, 1996). As noted in Chapter 2, the basic forms and conditions of this exclusion are dispossession of the means of social production; lack of access to urban and rural labour markets and opportunities for wage employment; lack of access to good quality or decent jobs; reduced access to government social services; lack of access to stable forms of adequate income; and exclusion from the apparatus of decision-making or political power.

Policy Reforms and Rural Development

Both the new and old economic models of rural development focus on three critical variables of the production and development process: (1) the existing stock and social distribution of natural resources, such as land (natural capital); (2) the stock of physical capital (i.e., the latest production technologies — and the process of technological conversion and productive transformation); and (3) the stock and supply of financial capital, and the rate of capital formation or productive investment.

Within the framework of the new economic model, facilitative policies include privatization of the means of production; deregulation of private economic activities and markets; and liberalization of trade and the flow of capital and foreign investment. With regards to agriculture, the dominant locus of economic activity in the rural sector, the critical policy has been the liberalization of trade, i.e., eliminating subsidies to local producers and any tariffs or other protective barriers, including preferred treatment to local producers such as non-commercial sources of credit.

Identifying the macroeconomic effects of these neoliberal policies on different strata of the rural population is no easy matter. One of these effects is suggested by evidence that agriculture is satisfying a decreasing proportion of domestic demand for food, which is, as Crabtree (2003: 144) points out, "a clearly worrying trend for a country in which a large proportion of the workforce is employed in agricultural activities." A clear policy objective of trade liberalization was to increase agricultural production and induce greater efficiencies in the process. However, the evidence from Peru, Ecuador, Bolivia, Mexico and elsewhere suggests that his has not occurred. Also, stagnant production and a decreasing domestic demand for food have their social correlates in the large number of rural producers that has been squeezed out of the production process, fuelling the immiseration of a huge and growing landless (and near landless) rural semiproletariat, the emigration to the urban centres of many of these semiproletarianized producers and the impoverishment of most of those who remain behind.

Between 1991 and 1994, at the behest of the World Bank and within the framework of a broad program of neoliberal policy reforms, the governments of Mexico, Ecuador, Bolivia, Peru and a number of other countries in South and Central America initiated an agricultural modernization law that among other measures included a derogation of the constitutional protection of communal property and provision of a legal entitlement to land worked by the smallholders and the near-landless. This allowed them to sell their land and, in the process, build a market in land as well as (supposedly) increase efficiency.

However, combined with the elimination of subsidies to local producers, the commercialization of credit, the reduction of protective tariffs and in many cases an overvalued currency, these measures, rather than resolving the agricultural crisis, created what analysts have termed a "difficult environment" for producers of tradable products, especially small-scale peasant producers (Crabtree, 2003: 144). The latter, Crabtree points out with regard to Peru — but the same pattern holds for other countries in the region — have been "extremely vulnerable to the inflow of cheap agricultural products." Not only has the increase in agricultural inputs and products undermined or destroyed local economies, forcing large numbers of producers into bankruptcy or poverty, it has accelerated a fundamental change in production and consumption patterns away from traditional crops, especially grains like quinoa, kiwicha, coca, alluco, beans and potatoes. The impact of this change and its implications for the livelihoods of the rural poor have yet to be fully evaluated.

In the case of Peru, the abolition of ECASA, one of a number of government marketing boards and agricultural price support institutions, liberalized the national market in rice, removing an organization that, like its counterparts in other countries in the region, had maintained price stability for the benefit of local producers. Some of the functions of ECASA were taken over by PRONAA, a government-subsidized food program for the poor that bought directly from small-scale producers. However, such an institutional change — replicated in the other countries in the region — had relatively little impact on the poorest farmers, many of whom had never benefitted from government programs of any sort (Crabtree, 2003: 147). The disappearance of Banco Agrario meant that those producers who managed to integrate themselves into the competitive local urban markets were forced to rely on agro-industrial firms for commercial credit. This credit, when available, was extended under onerous terms, with rates that in the case of Brazil under Cardoso reached 20 percent a month. The interest rates reflect the perception of high-risk involved in lending to smaller-scale producers. And creditors are extremely reluctant to lend, even to larger-scale, more prosperous landowners with privileged market access. Their appetite for lending is also reduced by the incidence of bankruptcies in sectors such as asparagus, which had briefly seemed to offer endless possibilities (Crabtree, 2003: 145, 147)

In many cases, the result of such institutional changes and recourse to "the market mechanism" has been a drastic deterioration in the situation of small producers, who are forced to sell their wares at prices below their costs of production, accrue enormous unpayable debts and in many cases are pushed into bankruptcy. In Mexico, this situation has generated one of the largest mass movements in its long history of land struggle, El Barzon — an organization of highly indebted independent family farmers. The peasant economies in Peru, Ecuador, Mexico and elsewhere in the region are devastated, with large numbers forced to flee the countryside in the search of wage employment in the urban centres. The only alternative was — and remains — poverty. Studies undertaken in this area point towards a pattern of increased social inequality and rural poverty: in the not atypical case of Peru, a decade of agricultural modernization brought about an increase in rural poverty from 41.6 percent of households in 1985 to 54.1 percent in 2000 (Crabtree, 2003: 148). The same study shows a pattern of decline in extreme poverty — from 18.4 to 14.8 percent — but no analysis or explanation, which can probably be found in the World Bank's approach to reducing poverty by statistical fiat.

Sustainable Development and Profits: Engaging the Private Sector

In the 1980s, the development agenda of international and nongovernmental organizations was to bring about a participatory form of sustainable development. A key component of the strategy pursued under this agenda was the inclusion of NGOs in the development process. These NGOs were formed for the most part in the wake of a retreating state — to assist the poor and their communities by mediating between them and the donors, the providers of development finance or technical assistance. In the 1990s, this strategy underwent a shift — to reach beyond the NGOs in the third sector (civil society) into the private sector (Mitlin, 1998) to incorporate profit-oriented enterprises and business associations the development process — "[to tap] the considerable resources, technology, competencies, creativity and global reach of the business community and employing these for development... goals" (Utting, 2000: 1).

The problem was to secure the participation of profit-making enterprises and transnational corporations in the agenda of sustainable development. The UNDP in particular defined and initiated the new strategy, which was laid out in a 1989 policy paper on the "U.N.-Business Partnership" (Palazzi, 2000; UNRISD, 2000).

Just as Bolivia, in 1994, took the lead in the design of a strategy of local participatory development, the Bolivian government proceeded to institute the sustainable development project of the international development community. In the first administration of Sánchez de Lozada ("Goni"), later deposed by the popular movement, the government institutionalized the development project in the form of administrative reforms, setting up ministries of sustainable and participatory development, and introduced enabling legislation. Another initiative was the setting up a directorate composed of representatives of national and provincial governments, civil society and the private sector (chambers of commerce and industry). The mandate of this directorate was to promote environmentally sustainable economic development and to do so on the basis of a partnership with the corporate sector, particularly firms that were "capitalized" (that is, privatized).

The workings of this approach can be illustrated by developments in the strategic oil and gas (hydrocarbon) energy sector, representing as it does a government priority with regard to national economic development. Within the framework of the government's strategic development plan and the broader agenda of the international development community, the key corporations in this sector, according to one of its spokespersons, "have assumed the environment problematic as a priority" (Arias, 2002: 47ff.). Manifestations of this priority, in the optics of the Bolivian Chamber of Hydrocarbon Industry (Arias, 2002: 46), include: (1) respect of international standards guidelines developed for the sector, as well as appropriate government regulations; (2) implementation of environmental impact assessments for all major projects; (3) environmental damage prevention and remediation measures of waste management, recycling and conservation; (4) setting up a division dedicated to R&D in the area of renewable (non-traditional) resources (green technologies); and (5) concern to mitigate the social impacts of corporate activity.

In addition to these principles, a critical factor in the implementation of a sustainable development strategy is popular participation — that is, the "participation of citizens and consumers" as well as "the growing role of NGOs" (Arias, 2002: 47). Bolivia, the Chamber points out, is not immune from these "global influences." Indeed, Arias notes, it exceeds most countries in "the velocity of these influences [vis-à-vis government reaction to them… legislation to regulate and institutionalize]."

This gloss on the government's approach towards the planning for sustainable development is symptomatic of the private sector's understanding of the meaning of the term partnership. The primary role of the government, Arias points out, is to establish a regulatory framework that provides "legal security" for corporate investors, particularly in regards to "serious short-term problems that are causing erroneous transaction costs to the companies, delaying projects and placing contractual commitments at risk." Second, the government has the responsibility of protecting private investors (particularly of the capitalized firms) from any liability arising out of the operations of these firms while part of the state. The privatized companies, on the other hand, have the responsibility to mitigate where possible the negative environmental and social impacts of these operations. Third, the government has the responsibility of mediating relations with the communities involved and perhaps negatively affected by oil and gas development. What this means is clarified by Arias in the following terms: "We are referring to the social pressures of those communities in areas influenced by oilfield projects." To wit: "Many times, the communities use illegal means and de facto measures to force the companies to increase damage payments or compensation (which should only be paid when they indeed take place and are proven)." At issue, Arias points out, is the lack of legal security for corporate investors relating to "the delimitation of native community lands and their ownership." The problem arises when "areas of hydrocarbon interest overlap protected areas," leading local communities to lay claims — and act — against the companies (49). The government in this connection, Arias emphasizes, is responsible for mediating relations with these communities and creating greater legal security for investors.

Although exploitation of hydrocarbons has the "potential to cause significant environmental damage and harmful social effects," at the same time, Arias notes, "it contributes in great measure to the country's development through employment, the generation of royalties and foreign currency, and tax payments" (48). The responsibility, and function, of government, in this regard, apart from the above, is to "define development priorities and to implement practices towards achieving these priorities in harmony with the policies [of sustainable development]." As for the private corporations, they "will respond to those signals provided they are clear and their application is transparent" (48).

The Illusions of Popular Participation

In 1994, Bolivia placed itself at the forefront of institutional reform in Latin America with the enactment of two laws — the Law of Popular Participation (Ley de Participación Popular — 1551, 20 April 1994) and the Administrative Decentralization Law (Ley de Descentralización Administrativa — 1654, 20 July 1995). With these laws the regime of Sánchez de Lozada made a conscious break with a political past identified with an over-centralized government and the social exclusion of the vast majority of the rural population, most of which belonged to an indigenous "nationality." Some observers considered Lozada to be embarking on the most challenging exercise in social reform since 1952, initiating thereby the most significant alternative project of participatory development in all of Latin America (Blackburn and Holland, 1998; Booth, Clisby and Widmark, 1995).

But not everyone agrees with this assessment. Some — for example, Arias (1996) and Medina (1996) — view this legislation as a radical response to social pressures exerted by the popular movement, a pragmatic attempt to respond to the growing demands by peasants and the indigenous population for increased political representation and autonomy. Others, such as McNeish (2003) and Untoja (1992), see in the laws an effort of the government to secure acceptance for its entire neoliberal agenda, including privatization. Still others see a response to attempts by the World Bank, the UNDP and other overseas development agencies to push for a participatory approach in the sustainable development process.

The hand of the World Bank and the UNDP in the design of Bolivia's plan for local government reform and municipalization is unmistakable (Bolivia, 1994). In this connection see, for example, the diverse appreciations of Palma Carvajal (1995) and Molina (1997). As these authors see it, the World Bank and the UNDP promoted a model of local participatory development ("municipalization plus popular influence") that combines: (1) the effect of decentralizing to local governments a significant share of government responsibilities/expenditures; (2) formal recognition of traditional social organizations of indigenous communities (as *organizaciones teritoriales de base* [OTBs]); (3) creation of an administrative apparatus for rural communities to participate in local development planning (popular participation councils [CPPs]); and (4) a partnership approach towards planning, bringing together representatives of the central and local governments (sub-prefect, mayor, surveillance committee) and civil society (peasant organizations, unions, association of OTBs and the civic committees). The aim in this process is to bring about sustainable local development in the form of a participatory planning approach and the concerted actions of the stakeholders and partners involved.

In this model, the municipality is recast into a key role to be played in new programs for administrative decentralization (Nickson, 1997). This new role is well illustrated in the government's decade-long efforts to institutionalize local participatory development in its planning processes (Bolivia, 1994; McNeish, 2003: 232–37) — to create thereby a complex of "productive municipalities" — and in its own analysis of these efforts (Delgadillo Terceros and Zambrana Barrios, 2002). In its report, the government focuses on the efforts to "construct a space for concerted action" (Chapter One) and the importance of the CPPs in "the formation of new local elites" (Chapter Three). As for "concerted action," the assessment report focuses on the civil society–state nexus, with direct reference to studies by the UNDP (PNUD, 2000, 2002) that identify the concertation of diverse interests as the greatest "bottleneck" in the development planning process. At issue, the report notes, is how to reconcile interests, which can — and do — come into conflict, and to concert decision-making and actions among the key sectors — civil society (citizens, NGOs, OTB, unions), the local government and the institutions (provincial development councils — CDPs).

The report adds that experience (in this "corner of Bolivia, one of the poorest in the country") points to difficulties in this area and a general failure to institutionalize the Provincial Council of Popular Participation (CPPP) — to secure this "concertation" consistently, notwithstanding the efforts to construct the required spaces for it. In other words, and without any sort of analysis or explanation, the report concludes that efforts to institutionalize the CPPP as a form of popular participation and concerted actions between civil society and the state have failed to bring about any concrete results. The report for some reason does not attempt to evaluate the outcomes and impacts of any projects decided upon within the institutional framework of municipal development planning — or the government's strategy of alternative participatory development (*desarrollo alternativo participativo*). Rather, its assessment is limited to the level of "participation" (consistency in attendance) of diverse actors in the planning process, which consists largely of meetings to hear reports prepared by the vice-prefect or a bureaucrat. Attendance at these meetings, the report finds, was consistently high — from 78 to 95 percent — in the case of community organizations and unions — inconsistently so (46 percent on average) in the case of the NGO representatives.

However, the report adds that this success at the level of participation did not translate into any definable gains, i.e., the institution of successful economic development projects. Nor has the government successfully secured the participation of some highly representative groups in the popular sector of civil society. The *cocaleros*, for example — an organization of some 30,000 coca-producers in the Chaparé region and los Yungas — refused the governments overtures to join in the participatory planning process. It opted instead for a strategy of mobilization and direct strike action — *cortas de ruta* (highway blockades) — to pressure the government to abandon its alternative development plan (to eradicate the highly marketable coca production).

In the face of this refusal, the government proposed the formation of a multisectoral directorate composed of local government officials and representatives of the *cocaleros* and private enterprise (*El Deber*, 9 December 2002: A14). The stated aim was to expand the scope for alternate production and a national market "structured on the basis of popular participation."

The *cocaleros*, however, the major participant in this struggle, responded that it was not in the least interested in "participation" as conceived of by the government; nor was it prepared to enter into a process of "negotiation and dialogue," an approach that has been tried before and "utterly failed" (*El Deber*, 9 December 2002: A13). Evo Morales, the leader of the *cocaleros* and a congressional deputy, observed that the private sector "does not have the slightest interest in participation," and he questioned the motives of the government. At a popular assembly, the key institution of the new sociopolitical movements that have emerged in the region (see below), the *cocaleros* resolved to continue popular mobilizations and direct action, seeking "strategic alliances" with other sectors to "massify" them (*El Mundo*, December 2002). This strategy was indeed acted upon, provoking government response in the form of a repression that left over a dozen people dead. The struggle continues.

So much for the government's strategy of popular local participation.

The Sociopolitical Dynamics of the Social Movements

Despite the efforts of governments in the region to incorporate them into the development process, social movements have generally opted instead for direct collective action, mobilization and struggle — and social transformation. In this regard, social movements can be distinguished from grassroots, community-based social or civil organizations as well as from the nongovernmental organizations that in partnership with bilateral and multilateral agencies dominate the development agenda. These NGOs, which in some countries exceed 10,000 in number, are the major implementing agents of the development project and the resulting process.

Latin America's experience with social movements and their history of struggle can be traced out in the form of distinct waves, each washing ashore in a specific conjuncture of objective (socioeconomic) and subjective (political) conditions. Four such waves can be identified.

The first wave hit Latin America in the 1950s and did not subside until the late 1970s. It took the double form of, on the one hand, a labour movement based on a largely urban struggle for improved wages and working conditions, and, on the other, a struggle for improved access to land and land reform. The context for these movements was complex but it included the Cuban revolution, which gave rise to pressures for revolutionary change, and widespread implementation of state-led liberal reforms and strategies to incorporate small-scale or peasant producers and rural indigenous communities into the development process. Governments co-opted, where possible, the leadership of indigenous or peasant organizations into development projects and repressed, where necessary, any rural or indigenous rebellions or movements for revolutionary change.

The second wave of social movements, roughly coinciding with the late 1970s to the mid-1980s, was composed of what were termed "new social movements" (Brass, 2000; Calderón, 1995; Calderón et al., 1989; Escobar and Alvarez, 1992). These included issue-oriented movements focused on human rights, the ecology, oppression of women and the ethnic struggle for autonomy, dignity of their cultural heritage and identity. In large part these movements were based on grassroots, or community-based, organizations and supported in their activities by the NGOs. The leadership of this form of civil society was largely composed of lower-middle-class professionals

(Dominguez, 1994), and their strategies revolved around challenging the military and civilian authoritarian regimes. The context for this wave was provided by a regionwide debt crisis, widespread implementation of the new economic model and the general retreat of the state from the economy, as well as a trend towards "redemocratization" in the form of decentralization and the return of constitutional regimes installed by democratic means, i.e., political parties and elections.

The third wave of social movements developed into a powerful political force as of the mid- to late 1980s. The context was provided by a process of globalization and the implementation of structural adjustment programs — a series of measures designed to adjust national and local economies in the region to the requirements of the new world economic order. This wave took the form of mass peasant and rural workers organizations engaged in direct action to promote and defend the economic interests of their supporters. The composition, tactics and demands of these movements varied, but they were all united in their opposition to neoliberalism (IMF-mandated policies) and imperialism (as globalization).

The most prominent of these movements include the Zapatistas of Chiapas (EZLN), the Rural Landless Workers of Brazil (MST), the *cocaleros* of Bolivia, the National Peasant Federation in Paraguay, the Revolutionary Armed Forces of Colombia (FARC) in Colombia — a relic of the social movements formed in the first wave and largely destroyed in the 1970s and 1980s — and the Confederation of Indigenous Nationalities of Ecuador (CONAIE). These movements, led by peasants or rural workers, have struggled for agrarian reform (redistribution of land) and national autonomy for indigenous communities, and they have struggled — and continue to do so — against globalization (in the form of ALCA, the Latin America Free Trade Agreement), neoliberalism (as government policy) and U.S. intervention, including coca eradication programs, colonization of territory via military bases, penetration of national police/military institutions and militarization of social conflicts, such as Plan Colombia and the Andean Initiative. The basis of these struggles was the neoliberal economic regime, the growing concentration of wealth in the hands of local and foreign elites and the social exclusion of the mass of local producers and their rural communities.

Unlike earlier waves of social movements in the region, the fourth wave has washed onto what Davis (2006) terms the "planet of slums" in the urban areas. It includes the dynamic growth of barrio-based mass movements of unemployed workers in Argentina, the unemployed and poor in the Dominican Republic and the shantytown dwellers who have flocked in the hundreds of thousands to the populist banners of Venezuelan President Hugh Chavez. The *piqueteros* of Argentina represent the cutting edge of this new wave (Petras and Veltmeyer, 2002).

In addition to the urban movements, new multi-sectoral movements that integrate farm workers and small- and medium-sized farmers have emerged in Colombia, Mexico, Brazil, Paraguay and Ecuador. The characteristic feature of these mass movements is an active search for strategic cross-sectoral linkages and alliances (see discussion below) and the concertation of urban-centred struggles. In many cases these movements are urban-centred but originated in rural struggles, resulting in the coalescence of two waves: the integration of movements formed in the third wave with those forming in the fourth.

The nature, mode of operation and style of political action of these movements challenge many of the stereotypes and assumptions of conventional liberal social science thinking and Marxist orthodoxy. For example, the "new social movement" writers declared the end of class politics and the advent of cultural and citizen-based movements concerned with democracy, gender equality and identity politics. However, the explosion of peasant and urban class movements throughout Latin America in pursuit of land and political power has shattered that assumption. The notion that the advent of economic and political liberalism would lead to the end of mass ideological struggles evaporated with the irruption of movements such as the EZLN and CONAIE. These movements and others have expanded and deepened the level and forms of popular participation. Each has become a mass movement. The elite and authoritarian civilian electoral systems (or democracies) are challenged by popular assemblies from below, which are in the process of defining a new substantive form of direct democracy. The defining feature of these new movements is a rejection of all traditional forms of politics (*Que se vayan todos!*), which has led to the speculative notions of "anti-power" or "no-power" by some scholars (Holloway, 2002) armed with a postmodernist sensibility about popular forms of resistance. In fact, the nature and political dynamics of these popular organizations formed in the fourth wave of social movements is not that well understood. The pattern of their evolution requires close scrutiny and further study. These new actors on the Latin American political stage have no script to direct their actions. Where these actions may lead, even what forms they might take in the immediate and near future, are as yet unclear and certainly not predetermined by the structure of their situation. I elaborate on this point in the concluding chapter.

Conclusion

The past six decades can be divided almost equally into two periods: one characterized by unprecedented system-wide rates of rapid economic growth and significant social advances both in the North and South of the world economic order; the other by a system-wide propensity towards crisis and diverse efforts to restructure a way out of this crisis. As a condition of this systemic and institutional restructuring, the changes, advances and gains made in the first period were generally — in some cases dramatically — reversed, bringing in their wake a highly polarized form of development, increasing social inequalities in the distribution of wealth and income, and the spread of poverty and other conditions of social exclusion.

Whereas developments in the first period, the era of development, were predicated on state-led reforms to the capitalist system of regulated and protected markets and on the political dynamics of populist or authoritarian regimes, in the second period, the era of globalization, they were based on the conjunction of economic and political forms of liberalization and liberalism — a marriage of convenience and convergent interests between free markets and open elections.

The new world economic order, created as a result of this new model, provides the policy and institutional framework for advancing the globalization project of the transnational capitalist class (Van der Pijl, 1998). The popular movement has mobilized the forces of opposition and resistance to this class project. In the context of a growing international or global North-South divide and under conditions of a counter-revolution and a new economic model, the projects of social transformation and development, which dominated the first period, both underwent a process of convoluted change. The former has taken the organizational form of sociopolitical movements that continue to challenge the system and the policies that support it. The development project, on the other hand, has been reconstructed in a number of different directions on the basis of a new paradigm that emphasizes the need for social inclusion, participation and sustainability (Rahman, 1991; Veltmeyer and O'Malley, 2001).

The key to substantive change — to move from social exclusion and poverty to development and social transformation — is for its proponents and protagonists to reach beyond both the state and the market into the popular movement and mobilize the forces of resistance in a new direction.

The development project is predicated on state-led structural reform and the reversal of policies designed for the corporate agenda of globalization; that is, capitalism in its neoliberal form is dysfunctional for the development process. To activate this process, governments should re-establish control over society's strategic resources and industries, regulate markets and private economic activity, and re-establish the public sector *vis-à-vis* the private sector and the institutions of global capitalism. In other words, the state needs to be restructured to serve the public interest — and escape the play, and power, of interests in the private sector of society. This type of change in the structure of political power and its state apparatus requires the mobilization of civil society in the organizational and political form of social movements and the concertation of these forces within a project of social transformation or systemic change.

There are two basic modalities of change and development within the popular movement: another development and social transformation. Both modalities and their associated political projects are at odds with neoliberal capitalist development and globalization. In the current context, there is no question about pursuing the path of social transformation in either the mainstream or on the margins of development thought and practice. It is possible, nevertheless, to identify a number of permutations in the search for an alternative form of development, including efforts to secure sustainable livelihoods of people in the rural sector. Despite (or perhaps because of) its *reformist* orientation, as well as its commitment to allay the negative effects of neoliberalism and the associated project of globalization and structural adjustment, the sustainable livelihoods approach (SLA) (Helmore and Singh, 2001; Liamzon et al., 1996), arguably, has the potential for bringing about an appreciable measure of improvements in the quality of life of the rural poor. The key to the sustainable livelihoods of the rural poor is the accumulation of social capital, a resource vested in the capacity to cooperate productively and form solidarity networks and that the poor have in abundance, thus requiring little or no change in the social organization of production — or, for that matter, in the structure of political power.

The reason that SLA might present the rural poor a workable option, an alternative to political confrontation and social mobilization, is that the political conditions for a revolutionary path towards development do not seem to exist anywhere, not even in Bolivia, where the popular movement has advanced the furthest. Protests against globalization and neoliberalism in the form of national policy is one thing, even where there exists the possibility of mobilizing the forces of resistance into a more or less united front, but to bring about the changes needed to open a revolutionary path towards development is altogether different. It would require a direct confrontation with the powerful forces of "economic and political freedom" (global capitalism and U.S. imperialism) and with the dominant ruling class, entrenched in the national structures of economic and political power throughout the region.

In the Latin American countryside today, the most dynamic forces of opposition to capitalist development in its neoliberal form — and of social change — are associated with a new wave of peasant-based and -led sociopolitical movements. But these movements do not have the organizational capacity or resources to mobilize other popular forces of resistance and opposition into a counter-hegemonic bloc — or, for that matter, to mobilize those few productive resources (social capital) that are available to the poor. A step towards substantive social change is provided by a strategy of horizontal inter-sectoral linkages and strategic alliances — what are termed "associative networks" — among diverse forces of opposition. However, the forces of reaction in Latin America's countryside and urban centres are formidable and likely able to withstand and stave off pressures for systemic or revolutionary change. Depending on one's politics this could be viewed as desirable or unfortunate. It is nevertheless inescapable.

On the one hand, the sustainability of rural livelihoods requires not only the empowerment of the poor via a mobilization of its social capital and the agency of civil society, but a substantive change in the existing structure of productive resources, i.e., access to society's wealth in its financial, natural and physical forms. On the other hand, such a radical or revolutionary change will not be brought about by the politics of local development. Nor will it result from the liberal reform measures of a developmental state. It requires a rupture in the existing structure of decision-making, the conquest of state power by the popular movement.

The problem that has thus far eluded the proponents of another development is that the sought-for empowerment of the poor requires more than palliative measures. It requires a confrontation of, and a fundamental change in, the existing structures of economic and political power. To decentralize responsibilities, policy-making and other forms of governance might open up some space for popular participation in decision-making. But it does so only on matters of local import and limited scope. The lives and livelihoods of the poor are greatly affected by forces of national policy and decisions made in the interests of those who own and control the major means of social production and who as a result dominate the national economy. The challenge for the proponents of another development — for the agents of social change and development in civil society — is to face up to this structural (and political) fact. In their failure to do so they might very well sow the seeds of collective direct action against the system that they are so concerned to protect.

Chapter 6

Social Movements versus the State
Political Power Dynamics of Social Change

Development requires change in the structure of class relations and the configuration of political power. The problem consists in how to bring about this change. This question continues to bedevil social and political analysts, notwithstanding the plethora of studies into, and decades of theorizing about, the dynamics of class struggles and power relations in different contexts and conjunctures. Also remaining unsettled are related questions about the organizational form that social change should take and what politics should be involved. Change at what pace and in what direction? On the basis of what agency and strategy? What *is* clear is that the road towards social change is paved with political power. Also the central issue remains the conquest by the popular movement of the state, the major repository of political power in regards to both the allocation of society's productive resources and of the coercive power with which to enforce its decisions and policies.

In terms of Latin American developments, it is possible to identify three modalities of social change and political power: (1) electoral politics — the pursuit of power on the basis of political parties; (2) mass mobilization, in the form of social movements, of the forces of opposition and resistance; and (3) local development, an approach to social change based on social rather than political action and associated with international and nongovernmental social organizations such as the World Bank and Oxfam. Improvements in the lives of the poor are brought about not through confrontation with agencies of political power but through the accumulation of social capital (the capacity of the poor to network and organize collectively). This concept of social capital is central to and defines the dominant approach towards social change in mainstream development theory and practice within the framework of the neoliberal model.

The electoral road to political power and social change requires conformity to a game designed by "the political class" and a non-confrontational approach that relies on dialogue, compromise and the institutional trappings of liberal democracy. Social movements, on the other hand, generally take a confrontational approach towards change and pursue a strategy of mass mobilization of the forces of resistance against the system and the political regime that supports it. Thus, the dynamics of social change are polarized between two fundamentally different approaches to political power: the electoral or parliamentary road, as it was once called, and the path of social revolution. The action dynamics of this political option — reform or revolution in the classical formulation — are not new. With diverse permutations they can be traced out across Latin America. What perhaps *is* new is the advance of a social, or non-political, approach — a new way of doing politics associated with the rise of grassroots, community forms of organization and local development — the dynamics of which form a central issue in political developments across Latin America today.

Neoliberalism and the Capitalist State

The neoliberal model is predicated on a minimalist state, the withdrawal of the state from the process of economic and social development and its replacement with the free market, a structure supposedly freed from the constraints of government regulation and other interferences in the normal workings of a system in its allocation of society's productive resources (to determine who gets what, or, in the language of economics, securing an appropriate return to each factor of production). Conditions for this retreat of the state emerged in the early 1980s, following the first round of neoliberal policies linked to the region-wide external debt and fiscal crisis. The first neoliberal experiments were led by military regimes in the southern cone of South America (Chile, Argentina, Uruguay), under conditions of a "dirty war" against "subversives" (trade unionists, political activists, etc.).

A second round of neoliberal reforms, implemented under conditions of "redemocratization" (the rule of law, constitutionally elected civilian regimes and the strengthening of civil society) allowed for and induced the widespread transfer of property, productive resources and incomes from the working class and the mass of direct producers to an emerging capitalist class of investors and entrepreneurs. With the popular classes experiencing the brunt of the sweeping structural reforms associated with the new economic model, widespread discontent spawned several waves of protest movements directed against the system. The neoliberal policy regimes became ungovernable, generating pressures to move beyond the Washington Consensus. The outcome was the construction of a new policy regime — a neoliberal program of macroeconomic policies combined with a new anti-poverty social policy.

Parts of this regime, such as administrative decentralization and a social policy that targeted the poor (as opposed to universality) for reduced public resources (a new social investment fund), were widely implemented in the 1990s. Other elements, such as the municipalization of development and a system of democratic, or local, governance based on the participation of civil society (stakeholders in the development process) were experimented with on a relatively limited basis, primarily in Bolivia (Palma Carvajal 1995; Ardaya

1995; BID 1996). These experiments constituted a third round of neoliberal policies but yielded few positive results in terms of economic growth and social development. By the end of the 1990s and into the new millennium, economic growth rates across Latin America were less than robust, a far cry from the prosperity promised by the World Bank and the ideologies of neoliberal capitalist development. Indeed, ECLAC, a U.N. agency that over the years has led the search for an alternative to the neoliberal model, was compelled by the growing evidence of sluggish and negative growth rates and a propensity towards economic crisis (in the late 1990s, after two decades of neoliberal reforms) to project "a new decade lost to development." Other erstwhile supporters of the new economic model were constrained to recognize the dysfunctionality of the neoliberal model and the need for fundamental reform of the reform process — to "move beyond the Washington Consensus" (Burki and Perry 1998; Stiglitz 2002).

As evidenced by country case studies (Petras and Veltmeyer, 2005) of Argentina, Bolivia, Brazil, Ecuador, neoliberalism as a form of capitalist development is not only economically dysfunctional but profoundly exclusionary in social terms and politically unsustainable. A decade of state-led reforms to the model has not fundamentally changed the Washington Consensus on macroeconomic policy. Nor has it changed the character of capitalist development in the region. Two decades of neoliberal reforms have resulted in deepening social inequalities, the spread of poverty and conditions of social crisis and disorganization. Even Carlos Slim, Mexico's major contribution to the *Forbes* billion dollar club and one of the region's greatest beneficiaries of the neoliberal reform process, has joined the chorus of negative voices levelled against neoliberalism, viewing it as not only dysfunctional in economic terms but inherently ungovernable. This conclusion, which a number of economists at the World Bank and other international organizations involved in the development project suspected all along, has fuelled a widespread search for "another form of development," a decentralized and participatory form of local development based on more sustainable forms of "democratic" or "good" governance (Blair 1997; Dominguez and Lowenthal 1996; World Bank, 1994). The result has been a veritable flood of proposals and alternative models for bringing about development on the basis of social capital, i.e., though the agency of self-help, or community-based, or grassroots organizations, with the assistance and support of partner institutions and international cooperation (Dasgupta and Serageldin 2000; Hooghe and Dielind Stolle 2003; Woolcock and Narayan 2000).

Social Movements versus the State

A decade of efforts to give the neoliberal reform process in Latin America a human face has failed. But what is needed is not a move beyond the

Washington Consensus towards face-saving and politically sustainable reforms of the model. Neither is a redesign of the structural adjustment program the solution. What is needed is a social revolution that will change class relations, property relations and the class character of the state. This conclusion is reached in the form of the following propositions.

> *Capitalism in its social and institutional forms is "the enemy," but in the current conjuncture the neoliberal state is the major locus of class struggle.*

State power is generally defined in terms of an "authoritative allocation of society's productive resources." But what sets the state apart from other institutions is control over coercive power, or, in the language of social science, its monopoly over the instruments of coercion and repression in its defined function of maintaining political order. The state has a range of powers but, as demonstrated by the review of state–social movement dynamics in this chapter, ultimately it is backed up by force. This fact has been well established in theory, and the social movements are all too aware of it in practice. In the cases of De Lozada and Mesa in Bolivia and Gutiérrez in Ecuador, the coercive apparatus of the state has been systematically directed against the social movements. In these contexts, state coercion has not been a matter of last resort or a justifiable exercise of state power, as viewed by so many analysts in the liberal tradition. Coercion or repression is part of an arsenal of weapons used by the political class to control the social movements — to weaken them in their struggle for social transformation. It is the range of powers that defines the relationship of the state to the social movements.

This proposition is confirmed by a review of the dynamics that surround the relationship between the state and the social movements in Argentina, Brazil, Bolivia and Ecuador (Petras and Veltmeyer, 2005). The authors concluded that the relationship of the state to social movements can be defined and is structured in terms of the following strategies:

- setting up parallel organizations to class-based, anti-systemic organizations, such as peasant organizations and unions, that have non-confrontational politics;
- repression of class-based organizations with an anti-systemic agenda where possible or necessary;
- dialogue and negotiating with representatives of class-based organizations with the capacity to mobilize forces of opposition and resistance (FARC in Colombia, MST in Brazil, EZLN in Mexico);
- accommodating the leadership of social movements to policies of economic, social and political reform, often with the mediation of NGOs;

- pacifying belligerent organizations on the basis of a reform agenda, a partnership approach and a populist politics of appeasement and clientelism;
- strengthening organizations within civil society that have a reformist orientation and a democratic agenda, and weakening organizations with an anti-systemic agenda, a confrontational direct-action approach in their politics; and, when all else fails,
- incorporating groups with an anti-systemic agenda into policy-making forums and institutions.

In the context of electoral politics, mass parties are transformed into parties "of the system" — pro-business and beholden to the Washington Consensus on macroeconomic policy.

The best case of this proposition can be found in the transformation of the Workers Party (PT) from a party of the masses into a party of big business. This outcome is the result of the long term, large-scale structural changes *within* the party and in its relationship to the state. The decisive shift in this case, as in the case of developments in Bolivia related to the Movimiento Hacia Socialismo (MAS), is from mass popular social struggles to electoral politics. In this evolution, the PT became an institutional party, embedded in all levels of the capitalist state and attracting as a result a large number of *petit bourgeois* professionals (lawyers, professors, journalists), trade union bureaucrats, upwardly mobile ex-guerrilla, ex-revolutionaries recycled into the electoral arena. What happens in these cases is that a process of substitutionism takes place. The electoral apparatus replaces popular assemblies, elected officials displace leaders of social movements, and institutional manoeuvres of the national political leaders substitute for direct action of the trade union and social movements.

The historical and empirical data demonstrate that elitist electoral leaders *embedded* in the institutional structures of the capitalist state end up competing with the other bourgeois leaders over who can best administer the interest of the foreign and domestic, agrarian and financial elites. But the fundamental change in the shift of mass parties towards electoral and institutional politics is found in its class composition: it tends to become the party of ambitious, upwardly mobile, lower-middle-class professionals whose social reference is the capital class. Political developments in both Brazil and Bolivia provide evidence for this assertion. Behind these developments can be found a change in class consciousness that reflects a change in the material conditions of the elected politicians. Depending on the capacity of these leftist labour-oriented politicians to garner voting support among the working class, landless workers and urban *favelados* become bargaining chips to negotiate favours with big business.

The "new class" of electoral politicians tends to look upward and to their future ruling-class colleagues, not downward and to their former working-class comrades. A similar development seems to occur inside the trade union movement in its relationship to the state. In the case of the Brazil under Lula, for example, upwardly mobile trade union officials look upward to becoming congressional candidates and ministers, or administrating pension funds, rather than downward to organizing the unemployed, and the urban poor in general strikes with the employed workers. The PT's transformation into a party of international capital was accompanied by the transformation of the major trade union confederation, the CUT, from an independent, class-based union into more or less an appendage of the labour ministry. The CUT followed the PT along the path of state institutionalization and "substitutionism" as the national leaders pre-empted the factory assemblies in making decisions and relocated activities from the streets to government offices. The parallel transformation of the PT and CUT avoided any rupture between them, a development that has not been followed in Bolivia. However, there are political forces in Bolivia that follow the Brazilian example.

The key theoretical point from this analysis is that the bourgeoisification of working-class, or socialist, parties is not the inevitable consequence of globalization. Rather, it is the result of changing class ideology and internal dynamics of party politics — changes that lead to institutional assimilation and, ultimately, subordination to the dominant sectors of the ruling class. This conclusion points to the profound limitation of electoral politics as a vehicle for social transformation or even consequential reforms. Social transformation is far more likely to occur from the direct action of independent, class-based social political movements oriented toward transforming the institutional basis of bourgeois state power.

Electoral politics is a trap designed to demobilize the forces of resistance and opposition

This proposition is amply demonstrated by political developments in every country case examined by Petras and Veltmeyer (2005), and particularly in Bolivia, Brazil and Ecuador. Many social movements, in their efforts to advance the struggle for political power, seek a strategic or tactical alliance with electoral political parties, as with the MST and the PT in Brazil, the CONAIE in Ecuador (Pachakutik) and MAS and Indigenous Pachakuti Movement (MIP) in Bolivia. In such alliances the social movements evolve into political instruments for the purpose of influencing regime policy within the system. This evolution is invariably at the expense of the popular movement, whose forces of resistance and opposition, rather than being brought to bear against the power structure, are dissipated and demobilized. No matter what their social base or ideological orientation, ostensibly progressive regimes with links to the social movements and neoliberalism inevitably became integrated into, and subordinate to, the imperial system. The result is that social movements and their members are blocked from achieving even their minimum goals. Pachakutik in Ecuador provides a good exemplar of this development, and to appreciate its theoretical and political significance we cannot do better than turn to Bolivia.

In the conjuncture of political developments that followed the indigenous uprising in Ecuador in 2000, the petroleum workers and CONAIE, through its electoral arm Pachakutik, entered into an electoral alliance with Lucio Gutiérrez and his Sociedad Patriotica. Catapulted into power on the basis of this alliance, Gutierrez, upon taking office, embraced privatization of petroleum and the policies of the IMF, Free Trade Area of the Americas (FTAA) and Plan Colombia. Gutiérrez repressed the petroleum workers and turned the government's back on the indigenous movement (betrayed it, in the conception of CONAIE at its National congress in 2004). The result was a much weakened petroleum workers union, a discredited Pachakutik and a seriously weakened and divided CONAIE.

In Bolivia, Evo Morales, the leader of the *cocaleros* and the Movement to Socialism (MAS), like so many electoral politicians and parties after some advances, turned to the right. In the wake of the October 2003 uprising, in which he was notably absent, Morales supported the pro-imperialist, neoliberal regime of Carlos Mesa, playing a major role in dividing and attacking any large-scale mobilizations in favour of nationalizing petroleum. The analysis by Petras and Veltmeyer (2005) of diverse electoral regimes suggests that this development is not in the least surprising. It is built into electoral politics, the inevitable result of its dynamics. In the case of Evo Morales, his politics was undoubtedly geared to his quest to win the 2005 presidential election, a prospect that many analysts saw as unlikely given the mechanics of Bolivia's electoral politics (the need for a second round of voting should no candidate achieve over 50 percent in the first round). But events in Bolivia proved these analysts wrong: Morales in December 2005 took the presidency in the first round, garnering 54 percent of the vote.

Political developments in Brazil suggest that no matter the electoral prospects, once a popular movement turns towards electoral politics it is constrained to play by rules that sustain the dominant model and, in the current context, the neoliberal agenda. The MST has not suffered the same debacle as CONAIE because only a few members were in the government and it managed to retain enough autonomy to maintain the loyalty of its members. Also, unlike the *cocaleros* in Bolivia, the MST is not dominated by a single electorally ambitious personality and is sufficiently grounded in class politics to avoid becoming a tool of the bourgeois state. Nevertheless, the MST's confidence in Lula and ties with the left of the PT have undermined its opposition to Lula's reactionary attack on pensions and minimum wages, the IMF pact and military support of the U.S. colonial occupation of Haiti. The danger here is that by continuing to give critical support to a discredited regime, the MST will suffer the same discredit, a lesson that CONAIE has learnt all too well.

Local development, designed as a means of eluding confrontation with the power structure and substantive social change, provides micro solutions to micro problems.

The best exemplars of this proposition are found in Bolivia and Ecuador, in part because of the indigenous factor in their national politics. In both countries, indigenous communities have demonstrated great capacity for mobilizing the forces of resistance and opposition, organizing some of the most dynamic social movements in the region. For this reason, the World Bank and the IDB targeted the indigenous communities and the social movements based on them as the object of what amounts to an anti-insurgency strategy: local development in the form of micro-projects of poverty alleviation.

Given the established dysfunctionality of the neoliberal model and the tendency of this model to undermine democracy and generate destabilizing forces of resistance, the architects and guardians of the new world order have turned towards local development (micro-projects) as *the* solution to the problem of ungovernability. The first step in this strategy was to establish a state-level institutional-administrative-legal framework. The next step was to enlist the services of NGOs, converting them into front-line agents of the "development project" and, in the process, into missionaries of micro-reform. NGOs provided the imperialist organizations cooperating in the development project entry into the local communities. The micro-reforms and NGOs promoted a pacific, or "civil" (non-confrontational), form of politics, turning the rural poor away from social movements towards local self-help projects funded (and designed) from above and the outside. They also created local conditions for an adjustment to the discipline of globalization and its governance requirements. As noted previously, Heloise Weber (2002: 146) wrote of micro-finance and micro-credit as a "coherent set of tools that may facilitate as well as govern the globalization agenda." With reference to these developments we can well conclude that the official discourse on civil society is little more than an ideological mask for an imperialist agenda — to secure the political conditions for neoliberal capitalist development.

Mass mobilization is the revolutionary way to power — the only way forward.

Political developments in every country case examined by Petras and Veltmeyer (2005) confirm what has long been a truism in Marxist class analysis. At issue in the class struggle is political power in the form of the state. Each advance in this struggle has been associated with mobilizational politics, while recourse to electoral politics in each case has perpetuated the status quo.

In no Latin American country are the conditions of a revolutionary situation as well developed as in Bolivia. At the time of this writing, the swell and rising tide of revolutionary ferment has abated, but this could very well be the calm before the storm to come, which is to say, Bolivia presents us with the possibility of a truly revolutionary movement with all of its trials and tribulations.

However, to advance the popular movement in a revolutionary direction certain conditions are required. First, the popular movement needs to coalesce around a powerful organization of insurgent forces. In Bolivia, the group with the greatest potential in this regard is the COB (Central Obrera Boliviana), an organization that has uniquely managed to both represent politically and advance the interests of both organized workers and indigenous peasants. A major source of the COB's political potential is its organizational structure, a single structure of affiliation at the provincial, departmental (regional) and national levels, with a demonstrated capacity for bringing together and concentrating the collective action and mobilizations of diverse sectors of the popular movement.

Notwithstanding its historical failures and limitations, the COB has the potential of constituting a critical mass of insurgent forces and mobilizing them into a movement that could potentially change the course of Bolivia's history. At issue here are three factors, in particular the requirements of organization, effective leadership and the construction of an appropriate and effective strategy and associated tactics. In this regard, the COB has to combine with other revolutionary forces, particularly those constituted by the Aymara indigenous proletariat of El Alto, organized by CTUCB (Confederación Sindical Unica de Trabajadores Campesinos de Bolivia) and under the command of Felipe Quispe. A second requirement is that the working class, led by the COB, needs to unite their struggle with the indigenous movement and the broader popular movement. MAS to some extent provides a political condition of such unity, the COB less so in that the it is precisely the division between different sectors of organized labour and the indigenous movement that has tended to and still divides the COB, weakening its political responses to the government's macroeconomic policy. A third requirement for the Bolivian revolution is for the base organizations and insurgent forces in the popular movement to break away from the system of electoral politics. This conclusion appears inescapable, but see the postscript to this chapter.

The prospect for these developments is difficult to gauge. Some observers see this as "not that difficult." Nevertheless, they recognize the formidable obstacles in the significant number of union and movement leaders who dialogue with the government within the framework of a social pact or support the electoral path followed by MAS. Others see an even greater obstacle in the diversion of the indigenous communities at the base of the popular movement into a politics of local "autonomous" development and their adhesion to an electoral strategy, not only in regard to the projected takeover of municipal government by MAS but the 2005 presidential elections. MAS is an important repository of oppositional forces but these forces are tied into the system via electoral politics of incremental reform. Thus, the social movement has to contend with not only the forces ranged behind the government but the demobilizing approach of a powerful political movement on the left.

The best if not only hope for the movement is for the rank and file to depose the leaders who are holding the movement back. For MAS this would not be so easy, or even possible, unless, as recently proposed by former MAS Senator Filomen Escóbar, in his battle with Morales, MAS is put under the control of a revitalized COB and thus subordinated to the broader popular movement as one of its major political instruments. But this scenario has various difficulties, not least of which is Evo Morales himself. Having chosen the electoral path towards power — the *toma municipal* in 2004 and the presidency in 2005 — he has not only abandoned the dynamics of mobilization (the revolutionary path towards power) but any pretension of being a socialist, let alone a revolutionary. He knows all too well that playing by the rules of electoral politics commits him to pursuing a capitalist path towards national development should he, as he very well might, eventually be elevated to state power. This is one reason why in October 2003 he swung to the right — to avoid any situation that might jeopardize the viability and survival of the institutions of the capitalist state.

As for former president Carlos Mesa, it is abundantly clear that he was not the progressive reformer that some made him out to be. Whether it is by ideological conviction, vulnerability to pressures from outside interests, ties to the dominant class or simply political ambition, he and his regime were fundamentally neoliberal. Mesa had not the slightest intention of negotiating the end of a neoliberal approach towards national policy, even if his government had been able to ignore the inexorable pressures exerted by the World Bank, the IMF and the U.S., i.e., the imperial state. Mesa's predicament, as he himself saw it, was how to balance these pressures and the requirements of good government (with sound policies, etc.) against the conflicting pressures of the popular movement.

It is likely that the contradictions that beset the existing regime will continue to generate revolutionary situations of one sort or another. The question is whether or not the revolutionary left will be able to respond to the challenge provided by these situations. While this remains open-ended, several things are clear. One is that it is critical to capture the greatest repository of political power, that is, the state. Another is that mass mobilization of insurgent forces — the revolutionary road to state power — rather than electoral politics, is the only viable method by which the popular movement can by its own actions bring about substantive social change.

Social movements fail to respond to the revolutionary challenge.

Marx a long time ago argued that capitalism in its advance creates its own gravediggers — a working class aware of its exploitation, disposed to overthrow the system. However, he noted, this development requires a revolutionary situation, the conditions of which are objectively given and subjective, structural and political. In several countries examined in this volume, particularly in Bolivia and Ecuador but also Argentina, these conditions have come together a number of times in diverse conjunctures: 19–20 December 2001 in Argentina, 8–19 October 2003 in Bolivia, and January 2000 in Ecuador.

To date in Brazil no such conjuncture has materialized. But at the same time, the presidential elections that brought Lula to state power did create the opportunity for a new regime to use this power to bring about a social transformation. But this would require a socialist regime and Lula's regime is anything but that. In fact, a socialist regime cannot take state power this way; electoral politics binds any party to the system, turning it towards neoliberalism — towards forces that govern the system. Thus, as in the other cases examined in this volume, the "moment" of state power — and the "opportunity" for mobilizing the forces of resistance against the system — was lost. In the case of Brazil, the reasons for this were predictable given Lula's politics and the class nature of his regime.

In Argentina the struggle for political power has taken a different form. The lesson that emerges from the extended and massive popular rebellion is that spontaneous uprisings are not a substitute for an organized political movement. The social solidarity formed in the heat of the struggle was impressive but momentary. Little in the way of class solidarity reached beyond the barrio. The parties on the left and local leaders did little to encourage mass class action beyond the limited boundaries of geography and their own organization. Even within the organizations, the ideological leaders rose to the top not as expressions of a class-conscious, organized base but because of their negotiating capacity in securing work plans or skill in organizing. The sudden shifts in loyalties of many of the unemployed — not to speak of the impoverished lower middle class — reflect the limitations of class politics in Argentina. The *piquetero* leaders rode the wave of mass discontent and lived with the illusions of St. Petersburg, October 1917, failing to recognize that there were no worker soviets with class-conscious workers. The crowds came, and many left when minimum concessions came in the form of work plans, small increases and promises of more and better jobs.

As in the other contexts studied in this volume the domestication of the unemployed workers movement is located in a number of regime strategies. Kirchner engaged in numerous face-to-face discussions with popular leaders, making sure that the best work plans went to those who collaborated with the government, while minimal offers went to those who remained intransigent. He struck an independent posture in relation to the most outrageous IMF demands but made concessions on key reactionary structural changes imposed by his predecessors. Lacking an overall strategy and conception of an alternative socialist society, the majority of the *piquetero* movement was manipulated into accepting micro-economic changes to ameliorate the worst effects of poverty and unemployment, without changing the structure of ownership, income and economic power of bankers, agro-exporters or energy monopolies. The resulting political situation, played out with diverse permutations across Latin America, was a variation on the all-too-dominant theme of local development and reform — and a politics of negotiation and conciliation.

The problem with this style of politics is that the question of state power is eluded. In the specific context of Argentina, it was simply a declaratory text raised by sectarian leftist groups who proceeded to undermine the organizational context in which challenge for state power would be meaningful. In this they were aided and abetted by a small but vocal sect of ideologues who made a virtue of the political limitations of some of the unemployed by preaching a doctrine of "anti-power" or "no power" — an obtuse mélange of misunderstandings of politics, economics and social power. The emergent leaders of the *piquetero* movement, engaged in valiant efforts in raising mass awareness of the virtue of extra-parliamentary action and of the vices of the political class, were unable to create an alternate base of institutional power for unifying local movements into a force that could confront state power.

What is clearly lacking in this and other situations is a unified political organization (party, movement or combination of both) with roots in the popular neighbourhoods, capable of creating representative organs that promote class consciousness and point toward taking state power. As massive and sustained as the initial rebellious period (December 2001–July 2002) was, no effective mass political party or movement emerged. Instead a multiplicity of localized groups with different agendas soon fell to quarrelling over an elusive "hegemony" — driving millions of possible supporters toward local face-to-face groups that lacked a political perspective. Under these circumstances the forces of opposition and resistance were dissipated, and the wave of revolutionary ferment receded.

Viewing these issues retrospectively leads us to the conclusion that is entirely consistent with the evaluation made by many activists within the movement: that it is a political mistake to seek state power from within the system — to turn towards electoral constitutional politics and join the government. This much is obvious. Assessments of the state-movement dynamic in other contexts have produced the same conclusion. The problem is that this conclusion does not get us very far.

Mobilizing the forces of opposition and resistance against the system is part of the solution — in fact a large part, given the limits and pitfalls of electoral politics. Indigenous leaders, like Humberto Cholanga of Ecuador, on the basis of struggles within the social movement, have embraced a class perspective on the "indigenous question." But another part of the solution is to create conditions that will facilitate the birth of a new revolutionary political party oriented toward state power. We can be certain that the process will be fraught with difficulties and will require the leadership of conscious political cadres. A close look at the experiences of the four countries provides answers to the limitations of social movements and electoral politics.

Prospects for Socialist Transformation

The socialization of the means of production and the egalitarian distribution of goods and services has been implicit and explicit among the rank and file of the mass social movements. However, the ritual declarations by the leaders of these movements of the vague slogan "Another world is possible" fail to define a political direction and economic strategy that links popular needs with fundamental economic structural changes. Faced with the growth of large-scale agro-export enterprises, agrarian reform can only be consummated through collective ownership and production — as the MST has recently acknowledged. The return of the financial elite in Argentina demonstrates that "regulation" is incapable of directing capital toward large-scale, long-term investment in employment-creating economic activity. Only through a publicly owned banking system, oriented by a regime based in the unemployed and employed workers, can employees and professionals design and implement financial policies that would develop internal markets. Hitherto, the "national" bourgeoisie, including those producing for the local market, have directed their profits to overseas accounts, recycled their earnings into the financial sector and/or intensified exploitation of their workforce, instead of expanding employment and reinvesting in the home market and technical innovations. The conclusion is that sustained and comprehensive industrial growth on a national scale requires public ownership under the control of employed and underemployed workers and professionals. The crisis of electoral elite politics — riddled with corruption, beholden to foreign creditors, immersed in the politics of privatization — can only be resolved by a transition to democratic collectivism, which prioritizes political control from below and internal investment over debt payments, and recovers the strategic sectors of the economy.

There is a growing popular dissatisfaction with the endless social forums, vacuous declarations and ritualistic self-congratulations that have become a substitute for organizing mass struggle based on a clear and expressive socialist program. Throughout five years of field work in the four countries with hundreds of unemployed and employed workers, in the formal and informal labour market, among downwardly mobile public employees and under-employed professionals, among Indian leaders and activists, the author and his colleague James Petras (Petras and Veltmeyer, 2005) found a much clearer option for a socialist transformation and rupture with the electoral political class than among the professional activists on the left who prefer to discuss the struggle for social change at diverse conferences (and the World Social Forum) than to support or join the struggles.

Conclusion

Historians of development theory and practice have written of a counter-revolution that can be traced back to the exhaustion of the Keynesian model of state-led economic development and the appearance of a "new economic model" based on the neoclassical doctrine of the free market as a fundamental engine of economic growth as well as the most efficient mechanism for allocating productive resources across the system, essentially replacing governments in this role. Other historians have identified a paradigmatic shift traced back to a "theoretical impasse" brought about by a structuralist approach towards social analysis and a political project to create a form of society characterized by a fundamental equality in social relations and equity in access to, and distribution of, the world's wealth.

As in Marx's day, these intellectual developments were analyzed by many as a war of ideas, a struggle by different ideas to realize themselves. However, as Marx understood so well in a different context, this conflict in the world of ideas reflected conditions of a class struggle in the real world, namely actions of working peoples across the world to improve their lot through a process of social change. The 1970s saw a new conjuncture in this struggle: a counter-offensive against the working classes launched by capitalists and their ideologues and state representatives seeking to reverse the gains achieved over two decades of economic, social and political development. The new economic model of neoliberal policy reforms was a major intellectual and ideological response, an important weapon in the war unleashed against the popular classes.

Another such response took the form of a sustained effort to disarm the popular movement, to disarticulate its organizational structure and class politics, and to turn it away from its struggle for state power and social change. The aim was to construct a modality for achieving social change based on a new way of doing politics, namely the path of "anti-power" or "non-power"; to rely on social rather than political action in bringing about social change; to seek change — and improvements within the local spaces available within the power structure; to partner with other agencies in the project of local development — to empower the poor to act in their own lives, participate actively on their own development and the good governance agenda, without challenging the larger structure of economic and political power.

The conclusion to be drawn from an analysis of this modality of social change and the political dynamics of the development project in Latin America is inescapable. The only way forward for the working classes and the popular movement is political power; to abandon the development project and engage the class struggle — to directly confront the holders of this power. However, as in earlier political conjunctures there are two roads to state power, both fraught with pitfalls: the road of electoral politics and a revolutionary politics of mass mobilization. Perhaps Evo Morales, the leader of MAS and erstwhile leader of the *cocaleros*, the coca-producing indigenous peasants of Chaparé, best exemplifies the dilemma (and the difficulties in pursuing both paths at the same time). Morales' decision to take the electoral road to state power (to bet on his chances of wining the 2005 presidential elections) was largely responsible for defusing the revolutionary situation created by insurrectionary politics of the popular movement in October 2003. Carlos Mesa would never have come to power without the support of Morales, who did not play a major role in the bloody street protests that forced Gonzalo Sánchez to resign and seek exile in the U.S., and the weak Mesa government would never have survived without Morales' support for the government's call for a referendum on the natural gas issue or without Morales' continuing support.

As Eduardo Gamarra (*The Herald* [Miami], January 15, 2005: 5A) noted: "The length of Mesa's tenure is largely due to Evo's supportive role." At the same time, Morales himself continued to be pressured from the left of the popular movement, compelled to respond to its more radical politics. For example, although Morales continued to insist that he wanted to win power only through the ballot box, in January 2005 he was constrained by the politics of the radical left to publicly demand that Mesa resign and call

114

an early election unless he rolled back gasoline price increases. At issue for Morales was how to maintain his position in the popular movement while standing on the sidelines of the class struggle during anti-government strikes that shut down the cities of El Alto and Santa Cruz.

Alvaro García, a university professor who is a part of the radical left but at times serves as an advisor to Morales (who has severed ties to most of the radical left), observed that "when the radicals are powerful he moves towards them." "The point is," he added, Evo "fear[ed] that he will lose his base of support to the more radical elements."

The response of Morales to radical politics tends to be tactical rather than strategic. It ties into a general conclusion that we have drawn from our analysis of diverse class struggles and the politics of social change. The inescapable conclusion is that a radical politics of mass mobilization is an indispensable condition for advancing the struggle for social change — to bring about a new world of social justice and real development based on popular power (control by working peoples of the state). In practice it is probably necessary to combine both electoral and mass revolutionary politics. But a mobilized people is the *sine qua non* of revolutionary change — and revolutionary change is the only way out.

Postscript

As predicted, Evo Morales achieved state power via the presidential elections in 2005. What does this mean in the light of the argument advanced in this volume about the pitfalls of the electoral road to state power? Not enough time has passed to draw any definitive conclusions or for us to revise our argument. It remains to been whether Morales as the country's president, as well as leader of MAS and part of the indigenous popular movement, will succumb to pressures arising from within the political class as well as global capital — constrained by the rules of electoral politics regarding the exercise of state power. It has to be said that thus far he appears to be responsive to the demands and pressures from within the popular movement. He appears to be moving further to the left in his policies than any other current leader in the region save for Chavez and Fidel Castro. Morales might even be paving a new road towards popular power and public policy, managing to escape or overcome thereby the pitfalls of electoral politics. But, as said, it is too early to tell, even at the time of this writing (November 2006), ten months into the new regime.

Some tentative lessons can be drawn. One is that the electoral process does indeed provide a road to power, perhaps more likely to bear fruit than social mobilization, which is fraught with even greater pitfalls, e.g., difficulties in bringing together diverse political groupings on the left. We have not examined the complex dynamics of left politics (associated with the so-called radical left of the political class) *vis-à-vis* Morales' road to state power but, to say the least, they have been politically divisive. Second, Morales' ascent to state power has had an almost transcendental symbolic significance with regard to the 500-year struggle of indigenous people in the whole region, as well as in Bolivia, against oppression and exploitation. Even though many in the indigenous movement, especially in Ecuador, are of the view that they are not ready for state power, they see that they nevertheless need to take the opportunity, as in the case of Bolivia, when it arises — as a means of political education if not substantive social change. The third lesson that can be drawn from Morales' ascent to power relates to the actual experience of state power, short as it is.

The issue of state power has both external and domestic dimensions. In terms of the former, the conjuncture has been propitious for forging a new set of strategic alliances with the presidents of Venezuela, Brazil and Argentina, in the direction of a common front against the U.S. and in forging a new policy regarding the exploration, processing and export of the country's oil and natural gas reserves: Bolivia has one of the largest reserves in the world, and a number of countries in the region, particularly Argentina and Brazil, are dependent on the supply of this gas and anxious to improve their access to Bolivia's resources.

Evo Morales has been able to push his nationalization agenda, in the form, on one hand, of declaring the oil and gas a state resource, and, second, of manoeuvring for a greater share of royalties and taxes, as well as higher prices for the resource, particularly in relation to Petrobas, the greatest foreign investor and player in Bolivian gas. It is not nationalization *per se* but rather a joint venture in which the state retains a controlling interest by means of a revived state enterprise and the regulation of foreign investment.

The domestic situation has already proven itself to be more complex than the international. Morales has spent most of his few months in office forming international alliances and agreements, in the region, especially with Chavez (Venezuela), Kirschner (Argentina) and Lula (Brazil), and also in Europe. These manoeuvres on the international stage, however, have had an impact on the domestic front. For one thing, they have consolidated internal support for his presidency and allowed for the accumulation of po-litical capital. Achieving power with just over 50 percent of the popular vote, enough to avoid the need for a second round, which he might not have won, his approval rate climbed to 80 percent (although it has since dipped), largely as a result of his politics on the international relations front (to explain and shore up international support for the nationalization and re-statification of oil and gas reserves). But Morales has not been derelict on other domestic fronts (apart from the issue of reprivatizing hydro-carbon resources), where he made several moves to consolidate the political capital formed in the electoral process. These included negotiations with the right-wing civic associations, dominated by private sector interests, to outflank the secessionist threat from the landed oligarchy and the bourgeoisie in Santa Cruz, the richest area of the country in terms of natural resources and economic activity. Another arena of internal politics has been in relation to his social base in the indigenous movement and its communities. One issue on this front has been that of coca eradication, a policy on which Morales has been steadfast in opposing pressures from the U.S.

Six months into his government, Morales faced active resistance to his policies in the form of an extended hunger strike by the coca producers of Los Yungas (his political base is among the larger group of coca producers of the Chaparé region). Another political front relates to organized labour, the most important player being the COB, although it might well be superseded by the new political formation, el Comando Nacional del Pueblo (The General Staff Command of the People), formed precisely because of the political impotence of the COB. This new political formation provides direct pressure on Morales from diverse sectors of the popular movement and the threat of mobilizing resistance against his policies should they stray to the right.

However, the most critical arena of political struggle relates to the macroeconomic economic and social polices disputed by the political class, reflecting dominant and entrenched economic interests. In this area Morales has thus far trod a fine line between concessions to the labour movement, for example, in the legislation of modest pay rises for public sector employees and workers, while maintaining the legislative and regulatory structure of macroeconomic policy put in place in previous regimes, as well as the guarantee of "legal security" to foreign investors and the multinational corporations.

What about the argument that we have advanced on social change and state power? The assumption behind this argument is that the road to social change is paved with state power but not in electoral form; even where state power is achieved via the electoral road, as in Bolivia, the left and the popular movement will ultimately lose because of the deals made in the process, accommodating the popular movement to the political class and forcing this class to adopt reformist (thus neoliberal supportive) positions at the level of national policy. It is too early to draw any firm conclusions on this point, but thus far policies adopted on both the external and domestic fronts provide few reasons for optimism. Changes on the social front have been limited. The new agrarian reform law does not entail a program of radical land distribution. What is projected entails little more than a new colonization project, opening up government-owned land on the agrarian frontier and leaving most large land-holdings intact. In cases of land expropriation the land is marginal and the owners are compensated at market values. On the labour front, the wage offer of the government to public sector employees in the health and education sector is a whopping 7 percent, leaving many to work for wages as low as $100 a month, barely above the poverty line,

The government is clearly constrained by the need to maintain fiscal discipline as well as political balance. At the same time, the popular movement has forced the government to place nationalization back on the political agenda, signalling a possible reversion in regional politics, the end of the privatization policy and a possible reversion to a new cycle of nationalization. This would be a significant political advance in both symbolic and real terms. It could even signal the beginnings of a new economic model and the restatification of the economic development process.

It is too soon to determine the broader significance of political developments in Bolivia and of Morales' ascent to state power via the electoral process. It has an indubitable symbolic significance for the indigenous movement. But its broader political meaning, particularly in regard to the use of the state apparatus as a means of bringing about substantive social change, is unclear. It remains to be seen whether Morales and the popular movement in Bolivia can escape the trap of electoral politics, although it is clear that the critical factor in Morales' ascent to state power was the combination of mass mobilization and an electoral process. And it is equally clear that the only way forward on the road to social change is for the popular movement to remain mobilized, to continue to exert the forces of popular mobilization on the government.

Acronyms

ALCA	Latin America Free Trade Agreement
BID	Banco Interamericano de Desarrollo
CASE	Research Centre for Analysis of Social Exclusion
CBO	community-based organization
CDP	provincial development council
CEPAL	Comisión Económica para América Latina
CEPR	Center for Economic and Policy Research
CFR	Council of Foreign Relations
COB	Central Obrera Boliviana
CONAIE	Confederation of Indigenous Nationalities of Ecuador
CPP	popular participation councils
CPPP	Provincial Council of Popular Participation
CSO	civil society organizations
CSUTCB	Confederación Sindical Unica de Trabajadores Campesinos de Bolivia/ Union Confederation of Peasant Workers of Bolivia
ECLAC	Economic Commission for Latin America and the Caribbean
EZLN	Zapatistas of Chiapas
FAO	Food and Agriculture Organization (United Nations)
FARC	Revolutionary Armed Forces of Columbia
FDI	foreign direct investment
FTAA	Free Trade Area of the Americas
GDP	gross domestic product
GNP	gross national product
GRO	grassroots organization
IDB	Inter-American Development Bank
IFAD	International Fund for Agricultural Development
IFI	international financial institution
IMF	International Monetary Fund
INEGI	Instituto Nacional de Estadística, Geografía e Informática
LSE	London School of Economics
MAS	Movimiento Hacia Socialismo
MIP	Indigenous Pachakuti Movement
MNC	multinational corporation
MST	Rural Landless Workers of Brazil
NGO	nongovernmental organization
NIC	newly industrialized country
NSP	new social policy
ODA	overseas development assistance
OECD	Organisation for Economic Co-operation and Development

OTB	*organizaciones teritoriales de base*
PI	portfolio investment
PIED	Programa de Investigación Estratégia en Bolivia
PNUD	Programa de Naciones Unidos de Desarrollo
PRSP	Poverty Reduction Strategy Paper
PVO	private voluntary organization
SCI	Social Capital Initiative
SLA	sustainable livelihoods approach
USAID	United States Agency for International Development
UNCTAD	United States Conference on Trade and Development
UNDP	United Nations Development Programme
UNEP	United Nations Environment Program
UNESCO	United Nations Educational, Scientific and Cultural Organisation
UNRISD	United Nations Research Institute for Social Development
USD	United States dollars
WHO	World Health Organization
WIID	World Income Inequality Database
WTO	World Trade Organisation

References

Albó, X. 1996. "Making the Leap from Local Mobilization to National Politics." *NACLA* 29, March/April.

_____. 2002. "Indigenous Political Participation in Bolivia." In R. Sieder (ed.), *Multiculturalism in Latin America: Indigenous Rights, Diversity and Democracy*. Basingstoke, UK: Palgrave Macmillan.

Annan, Kofi. 1998. "The Quiet Revolution." *Global Governance* 4 (2).

Ardaya, R. 1995. *La construcción municipal de Bolivia*. La Paz: Strategies for International Development.

Arias Duran, I. 1996. *El proceso social de la participación popular: problemas y potencialidades*. La Paz: SNPP.

———. 2002. *Los hidroarburos en Bolivia: Problemas y potencialidades*. La Paz: SNPP.

Atal, Yogesh, and Else Yen (eds.). 1995. *Poverty and Participation in Civil Society*. Proceedings of a UNESCO/CROP Round Table. World Summit for Social Development, Copenhagen, March.

Banerjee, Abhijit V., and Esther Duflo. 2003. "Inequality and Growth: What Do the Data Say?" *Journal of Economic Growth* 8 (3).

Bardhan, Pranab. 1997. *The Role of Governance in Economic Development*. Paris: OECD Development Centre.

Baron, S., J. Field, and T. Schuller (eds.). 2000. *Social Capital: Critical Perspectives*. New York: Oxford University Press.

Bebbington, Anthony, Michael Woolcock, Scott Guggenheim and Elizabeth Olson (eds.). 2006. *The Search for Empowerment: Social Capital as Idea and Practice at the World Bank*. Bloomfield, CT: Kumarian Press.

Behrman, J., A. Gaviria, and M. Székely (eds.). 2003. *Who's In and Who's Out: Social Exclusion in Latin America*. Washington, DC: Inter-American Development Bank.

Bessis, Sophia. 1995. "De la exclusión social a la cohesión social." Síntesis del Coloquio de Roskilde, World Summit for Social Development, Copenhagen, March.

Bhagwati, J. 1995. "The New Thinking on Development." *Journal of Democracy* 6 (4).

BID (Banco Interamericano de Desarrollo). 1996. Modernización del estado y fortalecimiento de la sociedad civil. Washington, DC.

———. 2000. Desarrollo: Más allá de la economía. Progreso económico y social de la América Latina. Washington, DC.

Birdsall, Nancy. 1997. "On Growth And Poverty Reduction: Distribution Matters." Remarks at the Conference on Poverty Reduction, Harvard Institute for International Development, February 8.

_____. 1999. "Life is Unfair: Inequality in the Global Economy." *Foreign Policy* 111.

Blackburn, J., and J. Holland. 1998. *Who Changes? Institutionalizing Participation in*

Development. London: Intermediate Technology Development Group.

Blair, H. 1995. "Assessing Democratic Decentralization." A CDIE Concept Paper. Washington, DC: USAID.

_____. 1997. "Democratic Local Governance in Bolivia." CDIE Impact Evaluation, No. 3. Washington, DC: USAID.

Bolivia, Ministerio de Desarrollo Sustenible y Medio Ambiente. 1994. *Plan General de Desarrollo Economico y Social: El Cambio para Todos*. La Paz.

Bombarolo, Félix, Luis Coscio Perez, and Alfredo Stein. 1990. *El rol de las ONGs de desarrollo en América Latina y el Caríbe*. Buenos Aires: Ficong.

Boom, Gerard, and Alfonso Mercado (eds.). 1990. *Automatización flexible en la industria*, Mexico: Editorial Limusa Noriega.

Booth, D., S. Clisby, and C. Widmark. 1995. "Empowering the Poor through Institutional Reform: An Initial Appraisal of the Bolivian Experience." *Working Paper* 32, Department of Anthropology, University of Stockholm, Sweden.

Bourguignon, F. 2003. "The Growth Elasticity of Poverty Reduction." In T. Eicher and S. Turnovsky (eds.), *Inequality and Growth*. Cambridge: MIT Press.

Bourguignon, Francois, H. Francisco, G. Ferreira, and Nora Lustig. 2005. *The Microeconomics of Income Distribution Dynamics in East Asia and Latin America*. Washington, DC: World Bank and Oxford University Press.

Brass, Tom. 2000. *Peasants, Populism and Postmodernism: The Return of the Agrarian Myth*. London: Frank Cass Publishers.

Brenner, Robert. 1998. "The Economics of Global Turbulence." *New Left Review* 229 (May/June).

Bretón de Zaldivar, Victor. 2003. "The Contradictions of Rural Development NGOs: The Trajectory of the FEPP in Chimborazo." In Liisa North and John Cameron (eds.), *Rural Progress, Rural Decay: Neoliberal Adjustment Policies and Local Initiatives*. Bloomfield, CT: Kumarian Press.

Bulmer-Thomas, Victor. 1996. *The New Economic Model in Latin America and Its Impact on Income Distribution and Power*. New York: St. Martin's Press.

Burki, S., and G. Perry. 1998. *Más allá del consenso de Washington: La hora de la reforma institucional*. Washington, DC: World Bank.

Burnside, Craig, and David Dollar. 1997. *Aid, Policies and Growth*. Washington, DC: World Bank.

Calderón, Fernando. 1995. *Movimientos sociales y política*. Mexico, Siglo XX1.

Calderón, Fernando G. (ed.). 1989. Descentralización y democracia: Gobiernos locales en America Latina. Santiago: CLACSO/SUR/CLUMT.

Camargo, Marcio, and Marcelo Neri. 1999. *Emprego e productividade no Brasil na decada de noventa*. Santiago de Chile: CEPAL.

Campbell, C. 2001. "Putting Social Capital in Perspective: A Case of Unrealistic Expectations?" In Ginny Morrow (ed.), *An Appropriate Capital-isation? Questioning Social Capital*. Research in Progress series, Issue 1, October. London School of Economics, Gender Institute.

Carothers, T. 1999. *Aiding Democracy Abroad*. Washington, DC: Carnegie Endowment for International Peace.

Carroll, Thomas. 1992. *Intermediary NGOs. The Supporting Link in Grassroots Development*. Bloomfield, CT: Kumarian Press.

CEPAL. 2003. *La inversión extranjera en América Latina y El Caríbe*. Santiago: CEPAL.

Cernea, M. (ed.). 1991. *Putting People First: Sociological Variables in Rural Development.* Washington/Oxford: IBRD/Oxford University Press.

Chalmers, D., C. Vilas, K. Hite, S. Martin, K. Piester and M. Segarra (eds.). 1997. *The New Politics of Inequality in Latin America.* Oxford: Oxford University Press.

Chambers, R. 1983. *Rural Development: Putting The Last First.* London: Longmans (now Pearsons).

_____ 1997. *Whose Reality Counts?* London: IT Publications.

Chan, Yu Ping. 2001. "Democracy or Bust? The Development Dilemma." *Harvard International Review* Fall.

Chang, Ha-Joon, and Ilene Grabel. 2004. *Reclaiming Development: An Alternative Economic Policy Manual.* London and New York: Zed Books.

Chhotray, V. 2004. "The Negation of Politics in Participatory Development Projects, Kurnool, Andhra Pradesh." *Development and Change* 36 (2).

Cibils, Alan, Mark Weisbrot and Debrayani Kar. 2000. *Argentina Since Default: The IMF and the Depression.* Washington, DC: Center for Economic and Policy Research.

Cohen, B. J. 1968. *American Foreign Policy: Essays and Comments.* New York: Harper & Row.

Coleman, J. 1988. "Social Capital in the Creation of Human Capital." *American Journal of Sociology* 94.

Cornia, G.A., T. Addison and S. Kiiski. 2004. "Income Distribution Changes and Their Impact in the Post-World War II Period." In G.A. Cornia (ed.), *Inequality, Growth and Poverty in an Era of Liberalization and Globalization.* Oxford: Oxford University Press.

Cornia, Andrea, Richard Jolly and Frances Stewart (eds.). 1987. *Adjustment with a Human Face.* Oxford: Oxford University Press.

Crabtree, John. 2003. "The Impact of Neo-Liberal Economics on Peruvian Peasant Agriculture in the 1990s." In Tom Brass (ed.), *Latin American Peasants.* London: Frank Cass.

Crouch, C., and A. Pizzorno. 1978. *Resurgence of Class Conflict in Western Europe Since 1968.* London: Holmes and Meier.

Crozier, M, S.P. Huntington and J. Watanuki. 1975. *The Crisis of Democracy: Report on the Governability of Democracies to the Trilateral Commission.* New York: New York University Press.

Dasgupta, Partha, and Ismael Serageldin (eds.). 2000. *Social Capital: A Multifaceted Perspective.* Washington, DC: World Bank.

Davis, Mike. 2006. *Planet of Slums.* London: Verso.

_____ 1984. "The Political Economy of late-Imperial America." *New Left Review* 143 (Jan-Feb).

De Ferranti, David Guillermo Perry, Francisco Ferreira and Michael Walton. 2004. *Inequality in Latin America: Breaking with History?* Washington, DC: World Bank.

Deininger, J., and L. Squire. 1998. "New Ways of Looking at Old Issues: Inequality and Growth." *Journal of Development Economics* 57 (2).

Delgadillo Terceros, Walter, and Jonny Zambrana Barrios. 2002. *Experiencias de los consejos de participación popular (CPPs).* Cochabamba: PROSANa, Unidad de fortalecimiento comunitario y transversales.

Diamond, Larry. 1999. *Developing Democracy: Towards Consolidation.* Baltimore: Johns Hopkins University Press.

Diamond, Larry, J. Hartlyn, J. Linz and S. Martin Lipset (eds.). 1999. *Democracy in Developing Countries*. Boulder, CT: Lynne Rienner

Dollar, D., and A. Kraay. 2002. "Growth is Good for the Poor." *Journal of Economic Growth* 7.

Dominguez, J. (ed.). 1994. *Social Movements in Latin America: The Experience of Peasants, Workers, the Urban Poor, and the Middle Sectors*. New York: Garland Publishers.

Dominguez, J., and A. Lowenthal (eds.). 1996. *Constructing Democratic Governance*. Baltimore: Johns Hopkins University Press.

Durlauf, S. 1999. "The Case Against Social Capital." *Focus* 20 (3).

Durston, J. 1999. "Building Community Social Capital." *CEPAL Review*, 69.

_____. 2001. "Capital Social, parte del problema, parte de la solución. Su papel en la persistencia y en la superación de la pobreza en América Latina y el Caribe." CEPAL website <www.eclac.org> (accessed Oct. 2006).

Eastwood, Robert, and Michael Lipton. 2001. "Pro-Poor Growth and Pro-Poor Poverty Reduction." *Asian Development Review* 18 (2).

ECLAC (Economic Commission for Latin America and the Caribbean). 1990. *Productive Transformation with Equity*. Santiago de Chile.

_____. 2002. *Statistical Yearbook*. Santiago de Chile.

_____. 2005. *Economic Survey of Latin America and the Caribbean*. Santiago de Chile.

Economist. 2005. "The Hidden Wealth of the Poor." November 5, Special Supplement.

Edwards, B., and M. Foley. 1998. "Civil Society and Social Capital Beyond Putnam." *American Behavioral Scientist* 42 (1) September.

Edwards, M. 2000. "Enthusiasts, Tacticians and Sceptics: The World Bank, Civil Society and Social Capital." *The Kettering Review*, 18 (1).

Edwards, Michael, and David Hulme. 1992. *Making a Difference: NGOs and Development in a Changing World*. London: Earthscan.

_____. 1996. *Beyond the Magic Bullet: NGO Performance and Accountability in the Post-Cold War World*. Bloomfield, CT: Kumarian.

Escobar, Arturo, and Sonia Alvarez (eds.). 1992. *The Making of Social Movements in Latin America: Identity, Strategy and Democracy*. Boulder CO: Westview Press.

Esteva, Gustavo, and Madhu Suri Prakash. 1998. *Grassroots Post-Modernism*. London: Zed Books.

Ferreira, Francisco H.G., and Michael Walton. 2005. "The Inequality Trap: Why Equity Must Be Central to Development Policy." *Finance and Development* 42 (4) December.

Finance and Development. 2005. "Latin America: A Time of Transition." 42 (4) December.

Fine, Ben. 2001a. *Social Capital versus Social Theory: Political Economy and Social Science at the Turn of the Millennium*. London: Routledge.

_____ 2001b. "It Ain't Social and It Ain't Capital." In Ginny Morrow (ed.), *An Appropriate Capital-isation? Questioning Social Capital*. Research in Progress series, Issue 1, October (special issue). London School of Economics, Gender Institute.

Foley, M.W., and B. Edwards. 1999. "Is it Time to Disinvest in Social Capital?" *Journal of Public Policy* 19 (2).

Forbes, Kristin. 2000. "A Reassessment of the Relationship between Inequality and Growth." *American Economic Review* 90 (4).

Fox, J. 1997. "The World Bank and Social Capital: Contesting the Concept in Practice." *Journal of International Development* 9 (7).

Fraga, Arminio. 2005. "A Fork in the Road: Latin America Faces a Choice between Populism and Deeper Reform." *Finance and Development* December.

Freedom House. 1999. *Freedom in the World: The Annual Survey of Political Rights and Civil Liberties 1998–1999*. New York: Freedom House.

Friedmann, John. 1992. *Empowerment: The Politics of Alternative Development*. Cambridge: Blackwell.

Ghai, Dharam. 1991. *The IMF and the South: The Social Impact of Crisis and Adjustment*. London: Zed Books.

Gideon J. 1998. "The Politics of Social Service Provision through NGOs: A Study of Latin America." *Bulletin of Latin American Research* 17 (3).

Gittell, R., and V. Vidal. 1998. *Community Organizing: Building Social Capital as a Development Strategy*. Thousand Oaks, CA: Sage Publications.

Glaeser, E.L. 2001. "The Formation of Social Capital." *Canadian Journal of Policy Research* 2 (1).

Goetz, A.M. 1996. "Who Takes the Credit? Gender Power and Control over Loan Use in Rural Credit Programmes in Bangladesh." *World Development* 24 (1).

Gonzales de la Rocha, M. 1994. *The Resources of Poverty*. Oxford: Blackwell.

Gonzalez Amador, Roberto, and Rosa Vargas. 2005. "Baja pobreza rural pero crece desigualdad." *Demos, Desarrollo de Medios*, S.A. de C.V., August 25.

Goss, Sue. 2001. *Making Local Governance Work: Networks, Relationships and the Management of Change*. New York: Palgrave.

Grootaert, C. 1998. "Social Capital: The Missing Link?" *Social Capital Initiative Working Paper*, No. 3. Washington, DC: The World Bank Social Development Family Environmentally and Socially Sustainable Development Network.

Grootaert, C., and T. van Bastelaer. 2002. "Understanding and Measuring Social Capital: A Synthesis of Findings and Recommendations from the Social Capital Initiative." Forum Series on the Role of Institutions in Promoting Economic Growth, January 11. Washington, DC: World Bank.

Guimaraes, Roberto. 1989. *Desarrollo con equidad: ¿un nuevo cuento de hadas para los años de noventa?* LC/R. 755. Santiago de Chile: CEPAL.

Gwin, Catherine, and Joan M. Nelson. 1997. *Perspectives on Aid and Development*. Washington, DC: Overseas Development Council.

Haggard, S., and R. Kaufman. 1995. *The Political Economy of Democratic Transitions*. Princeton, NJ: Princeton University Press.

Hanmer, L., and D. Booth. 2001. "Pro-Poor Growth: Why Do We Need It?" Mimeo. London: Overseas Development Institute.

Harris, J. 2001. *Depoliticising Development: The World Bank and Social Capital*. New Delhi: Left Word Books.

Harris, J., and P. de Renzio. 1997. "Policy Arena: 'Missing Link' or Analytically Missing? The Concept of Social Capital: An Introductory Bibliographic Essay." *Journal of International Development* 9 (7).

Hayden, Robert. 2002. "Dictatorships of Virtue." *Harvard International Review* Summer.

Hayter, Teresa. 1971. *Aid as Imperialism*. Harmondsmouth: Penguin Books.

Helmore, Kristen, and Naresh Singh. 2001. *Sustainable Livelihoods: Building on the Wealth of the Poor.* West Hartford, CT: Kumarian Press.

Hilhorst, Dorothea. 2003. *The Real World of NGOs.* London: Zed Books.

Hirsch, Joachim. 2003. "The State's New Clothes: NGOs and the Internationalization of States." *Rethinking Marxism,* 15 (2).

Holloway, John. 2002. *Change the World without Taking Power: The Meaning of Revolution Today.* London: Pluto Press.

Hooghe, Marc, and Dietlind Stolle (eds.). 2003. *Generating Social Capital: Civil Society and Institutions in Comparative Perspective.* New York: Palgrave.

Huntington, S.P. 1991. *The Third Wave Democratization in the Late Twentieth Century.* Norman: University of Oklahoma Press.

Huntington, Samuel, Micher Crozier and Joji Watanuki. 1975. *The Crisis of Democracy: A Report [No. 8] to the Trilateral Commission.* New York: Penquin.

IDB (Inter-American Development Bank). 1998. *Economic and Social Progress in Latin America: Facing Up to Inequality.* Washington, DC.

IFAD (International Fund for Agricultural Development). 1998. *PROZACHI: La historia de un proyecto para el desarrollo de pequeños productores en Zacapa y Chiquimula.* Rome.

_____. 2002. *Strategy for Rural Poverty Reduction in Latin America and the Caribbean.* Available at <http://www.ifad.org/operations/regional/2002/pl/pl.htm> (accessed Dec. 2006).

INEGI (Instituto Nacional de Estadística, Geografía e Informática. 2004. *Estadísticas Sociodemograficas.* Mexico City: INEGI.

Jazairy, Idriss, Mohiuddin Alamgir and Theresa Panuccio. 1992. *The State of World Rural Poverty.* London: Intermediate Technology Publications (for the International Fund for Agricultural Development).

Judis, J.B. 2004. "Imperial Amnesia." *Foreign Policy* July/August.

Kakwani, N., and E.M. Pernia. 2000. "What is Pro-Poor Growth?" *Asian Development Review* 18 (1).

Kamat, Sangeeta. 2003. "NGOs and the New Democracy: The False Saviours of International Development." *Harvard International Review* Spring.

Kapstein, Ethan. 1996. "Workers and the World Economy." *Foreign Affairs* 75, (3).

Karl, T.L. 2000. "Economic Inequality and Democratic Instability." *Journal of Democracy* XI (1).

Katz, J. (ed.). 1996. "Estabilización macroeconómica, reforma estructural y comportamiento industrial. Estructura y funcionamiento del sector manufecturero Latinoamericano en los años 90." Buenos Aires: Alianza Editorial.

Kaufmann, Daniel, Art Kraay and Pablo Zoido-Lobatón. 1999. *Governance Matters.* Washington, DC: World Bank.

Kawachi, I., B. Kennedy and K. Lochner. 1997. "Long Live Community: Social Capital as Public Health." *The American Prospect* 35, November-December.

Klasen, S. 2000. "Measuring Poverty and Deprivation in South Africa." *Review of Income and Wealth* 42 (1).

_____. 2003. "In Search of the Holy Grail: How to Achieve Pro-Poor Growth." In L. Kolstad, B. Tungodden and N. Stern (eds.), *Towards Pro-Poor Policies.* Proceedings from the ABCDE Europe Conference. Washington, DC.

_____. 2005. "Economic Growth and Poverty Reduction: Measurement and Policy Issues." Paper (Final Draft) for POVNET—Work Program on Pro-Poor Growth, February 5.

Kliksberg, B. (ed.). 1997. *Pobreza. Un tema impostergable. Nuevas respuestas a nivel mundial.* Mexico City: Fondo de Cultura Económica (FCEW).

_____. 1999a. "Desigualdad y desarrollo en América Latina. El debate postergado." *Reforma y Democracia* 14. Caracas: Latin American Centre for Development Administration (CLAD).

_____. 1999b. "Social Capital and Culture: Master Keys to Development." *CEPAL Review* 69 (December).

_____. 2001. "Seis tesis no convencionales sobre participación." In Bernardo Kliksberg and Luciano Tomasini (eds.), *Capital social y cultura: Claves estrategícos para el desarrollo.* Buenos Aires: BID-Fondo Cultural Económico

Knack, S. 1999. "Social Capital, Growth and Poverty: A Survey of Cross-Country Evidence." *Social Capital Initiative Working Paper* 7. Washington, DC: World Bank, Social Development Department.

Knack, S., and P. Keefer. 1997. "Does Social Capital have an Economic Payoff? A Cross-country Investigation." *Quarterly Journal of Economics* CXII (4).

Kohli, A. 1995. *Democracy and Discontent.* Cambridge: Cambridge University Press.

Krueger, Anne, C. Michalopoulos and V. Ruttan. 1989. *Aid and Development.* Baltimore: Johns Hopkins University Press.

Krugman, Paul. 2006. "México y el modelo neoliberals." *La Jornada* March 3: A7.

Kuczynski, Pedro-Pablo, and John Williamson (eds.). 2003. *After the Washington Consensus: Restarting Growth and Reform in Latin America.* Washington, DC: Institute for International Economics.

Kundnani, Hans. 2006. "Rich get even richer in Third World." *Guardian Weekly*, June 30–July 6.

Leffler, Melvyn. 2004. "Bush's Foreign Policy." *Foreign Policy* September–October.

Liamzon, Tina. (ed.). 1996. *Towards Sustainable Livelihoods.* Rome: Society for International Development.

Lindenberg, Mark, and Coralie Bryant. 2002. *Going Global: Transforming Relief and Development NGOs.* Bloomfield, CT: Kumarian.

Londoño, J.L. 1996. *Pobreza, desigualdad y formación del capital humano en América Latina.* Washington, DC: World Bank.

Lopez , Humberto. 2004. *Pro-Poor Growth: A Review of What We Know (and of What We Don't).* Washington, DC: World Bank.

Lotze, Conny. 2005. "Economics with a Social Face." *Finance and Development* 42 (4), December.

Lozana, Claudio. 2006. *La dueda interna se acentua: Ingresos, salarios y convenios colectivos en Argentina 2006.* Buenos Aires: ArgenPress.

Lustig, Nora, and Omar Arias. 2000. "Poverty Reduction." *Finance and Development* 37 (1) March.

Lustig, Nora, and Michael Walton. 1999. "Crises and the Poor: A Template for Action." Inter-American Development Bank Conference on Social Protection and Poverty, February.

Marglin, Stephen, and Juliet Schor (eds.). 1990. *The Golden Age of Capitalism: Reinterpreting the Postwar Experience.* Oxford: Clarendon Press.

Max-Neef, Manfred, Antonio Elizalde and Martin Hopenhayen. 1965. "Desarrollo a Escala Humana: una opcion para el futoro." *Development Dialogue*, Special Number. Dag Hammarskjold Foundation.

Mayorga, René. 1997. "Bolivia's Silent Revolution." *Journal of Democracy*, 8 (1).

Mayoux, L. 2001. "Tackling the Down Side: Social Capital, Women's Empowerment and West African Micro-Finance." *Development and Change* 32 (3).

McCulloch, N., and B. Baulch. 1999. "Tracking Pro-Poor Growth." *ID21 Insights*, 31. Sussex: Institute of Development Studies.

McLean, Scott, David A. Scholtz and Manfred Steger. (eds.). 2002. *Social Capital: Critical Perspectives on Community and Bowling Alone*. New York: New York University Press.

McNeish, John. 2003. "Globalization and the Reinvention of Andean Tradition: The Politics of Community and Ethnicity in Highland Bolivia." In Tom Brass (ed.), *Latin American Peasants*. London: Frank Cass.

Medina, Javier. 1996. *La participación popular como fruto de las luchas sociales en Bolivia*. La Paz: Ministerio de Desarrollo Humano.

Mitlin, Diana. 1998. "The NGO Sector and Its Role in Strengthening Civil Society and Securing Good Governance." In Armanda Bernard, Henry Helmich and Percy Lehning (eds.), *Civil Society and International Development*. Paris: OECD Development Centre.

Mokhiber, Russel, and Robert Weissman. 2001. "Corporate Globalization and the Poor." Available at <corp-focus-admin@lists.essential.org> (accessed August 6, 2006).

Molina, M. Fernando. 1997. *Historia de la participación popular*. La Paz: Ministerio de Desarrollo Humano.

Molyneux, M. 2002. "Social Capital: a Post-Transition Concept? Questions of Context and Gender from a Latin American Perspective." *Development and Change* Spring.

Morley, Samuel. 1995. "Structural Adjustment and Determinants of Poverty in Latin America." In Nora Lustig (ed.), *Coping with Austerity: Poverty and Inequality in Latin America*. Washington, DC: Brookings Institute.

Moronto, Adam. 2004. "The Antiglobalization Movement: Juggernaut or Jalopy?" In H. Veltmeyer (ed.), *Globalization/Antiglobalization*. Aldershot, UK: Ashgate.

Morrow, Ginny (ed.). 2001. *An Appropriate Capital-isation? Questioning Social Capital*. Research in Progress Series, Issue 1, October (special issue). London School of Economics, The Gender Institute.

Mosley, P. 1999. "Globalization, Economic Policy and Growth Performance." *International Monetary and Financial Issues for the 1990s* X: 157–74. New York and Geneva: United Nations.

Narayan, Deepa. 2002. *Empowerment and Poverty Reduction: A Sourcebook*. Washington, DC: World Bank.

Nickson, R.A. 1997. *Local Government in Latin America*. New York: Lynne Rienner Publications.

OECD (Organisation for Economic Co-operation and Development). 1997. *Final Report of the DAC Ad Hoc Working Group on Participatory Development and Good Governance*. Paris.

Ostry, Silvia. 1990. *Government and Corporations in a Shrinking World: Trade and Innovation Policies in the US, Europe and Japan*. New York: Council on Foreign Relations.

Ottaway, Marina. 2003. *Democracy Challenged: The Rise of Semi-Authoritarianism*. Washington, DC: Carnegie Endowment for International Peace.

Palazzi, Marcello. 2000. "Business-Municipality Partnerships." *Global Futures Bulletin* 120, November 15.

Palma Carvajal, Eduardo. 1995. "Decentralization and Democracy: The New Latin American Municipality." *CEPAL Review* 55.

Paugam, Serge (ed.). 1996. *L' exclusion. L'Etat des savoirs.* Paris: Ed. La Découverte.

Petras, J., and H. Veltmeyer. 2001. *Unmasking Globalization: The New Face of Imperialism.* London: Zed Books; Halifax: Fernwood Books.

_____. 2002. *Argentina: Entre desintegración y la revolución.* Buenos Aires: Editorial la Maza.

_____. 2005. *Social Movements and the State: Argentina, Bolivia, Brazil, Ecuador.* London: Pluto Press.

PNUD (Programa de Naciones Unidos de Desarrollo). 2000. *Informe de Desarrollo Humano.* La Paz: PNUD.

_____. 2002. *Informe de Desarrollo Humano.* La Paz.

Portes, A. 1998. "Social Capital: its Origins and Applications in Modern Sociology." *Annual Review of Sociology* 24.

Pochmann, Marcio (ed.). 2004. *Atlas da exclusâo no mundo.* 5 vols. Sao Paulo: Cortez Editora.

Portes, A., and P. Landolt. 1996. "The Downside of Social Capital." *The American Prospect* 7 (26) May/June.

_____. 2000. "Social Capital: Promise and Pitfalls of its Role in Development." *Journal of Latin American Studies* 32.

Psacharopoulos, George, and H.A. Patrinos (eds.). 2004. *Indigenous People and Poverty in Latin America; An Empirical Analysis.* Washington, DC: World Bank.

Putnam, R.D. 1993. *Making Democracy Work.* Princeton, NJ: Princeton University Press.

_____. 1995. "Tuning In, Tuning Out: The Strange Disappearance of Social Capital in America." *Political Science and Politics* 28.

_____. 2000. *Bowling Alone: The Collapse and Revival of American Community.* New York: Simon and Schuster.

_____ (ed.). 2002. *Democracy in Flux: The Evolution of Social Capital in Contemporary Society.* New York: Oxford University Press.

Putzel, J. 1997. "Accounting for the Dark Side of Social Capital: Reading Robert Putnam on Democracy." *Journal of International Development* 8 (7).

Rahman, Anisur. 1991. "Towards an Alternative Development Paradigm." *IFDA Dossier* 81, April-June.

Rao, V. 2002. "Community Driven Development: A Brief Review of the Research." World Bank, Washington, DC.

Rapley, John. 2004. *Globalization and Inequality: Neoliberalism's Downward Spiral.* Boulder, CO: Lynne Reinner.

Ravallion, Martin. 2004. *Pro-Poor Growth: A Primer.* Washington, DC: World Bank, Development Research Group.

Ravallion, M., and S. Chen. 2003. "Measuring Pro-Poor growth." *Economic Letters* 78 (1).

Razeto, L. 1988. *Economía de solidaridad y mercado democratico,* Vol. III. Santiago: PET, Academia de Humanismo Cristiano.

_____. 1993. *De la economia popular a la economia de solidaridad en un proyecto de desarrollo alternativo.* Santiago: Programa de Economía del Trabajo (PET).

Reilly, Charles. 1989. *The Democratisation of Development: Partnership at the Grassroots.* Arlington, VA: Inter-American Foundation Annual Report.

Retolaza Eguren, Iñigo. 2003. "El municipio somos todos. Gobernancia participativa y transferencia municipal." *Medicus Mundi.* La Paz: Editorial Plural.

Rice, J., and M. Prince. 2000. "Civil Society and Community Capacity: Links Between Social Policy and Social Capital." In *Changing Politics of Canadian Social Policy.* Toronto: University of Toronto Press.

Riddell, Roger, and Mark Robinson. 1997. *NGOs and Rural Poverty Alleviation.* London: Overseas Development Institute.

Robinson, Lindon, and Marcelo Siles. Social Capitalism Institute Website: <www.msu.ed/news/decjan02.pdf> (accessed Nov. 2006).

Rodrik, Dani. 1995. "Why Is There Multilateral Lending?" In Michael Bruno and Boris Pleskovic (eds.), *Annual World Bank Conference on Development Economics.* Washington, DC: World Bank.

_____. 1997. *Has Globalization Gone Too Far?* Institute for International Economics, Harvard University.

_____. 2002. "After Neo-Liberalism, What?" *Economic Times*, November 19.

Rondinelli, D.A. 1989. "Implementing Decentralization Programs in Asia: A Comparative Analysis." *Public Administration and Development* 3 (3): 181–207.

Rondinelli, D.A., J. McCullough and W. Johnson. 1989. "Analyzing Decentralization Policies in Developing Countries: A Political Economy Framework." *Development and Change* 20 (1).

Rondinelli, D.A., J.R. Nellis and G.S. Cheema. 1983. "Decentralization in Developing Countries: A Review of Recent Experience." *World Bank Staff Paper,* No. 581. Washington, DC: World Bank.

Rueschmeyer, D., and E.H. Stephens. 1992. *Capitalist Development and Democracy.* Chicago: University of Chicago Press.

Saavedra, Jaime, and Omar Arias. 2005. "Stuck in a Rut." *Finance and Development* 42 (4), December.

Sachs, Wolfgang (ed.). 1992. *The Development Dictionary: A Guide to Knowledge and Power.* London: Zed Books.

Salbuchi, Adrian. 2000. *El cerebro del mundo: La cara oculta de la globalización.* Córdoba: Ediciones del Copista.

Salop, Joanne. 1992. "Reducing Poverty: Spreading the Word." *Finance and Development* 29 (4) December.

Sampson, R.J. 1991. "Linking the Micro- and Macro-Level Dimensions of Community Social Organisation." *Social Forces* 70 (1).

Sánchez, Rolando (ed.). 2003. *Desarrollo pensado desde los municipios: Capital social y despliegue de potencialidades local.* La Paz: PIED (Programa de Investigación Estratégia en Bolivia).

Saxe-Fernández, John. 2002. *La Compra Venta de México.* Mexico: Plaza Janes.

Saxe-Fernández, John, and Omar Núñez. 2001. "Globalización e Imperialismo: La transferencia de Excedentes de América Latina." In Saxe-Fernández et al., eds. *Globalización, Imperialismo y Clase Social.* Buenos Aires/México: Editorial Lúmen.

Schulman, M.D., and C. Anderson. 1999. "The Dark Side of the Force: A Case Study of Restructuring and Social Capital." *Rural Sociology* 64 (3).

Schuurman, F. (ed.). 1993. *Beyond the Impasse: New Directions in Development Theory.* London: Zed Books.

Seabrook, Jeremy. 2006. "In a World of Wealth, Poverty has become a Necessity." *The Guardian,* July 27.

SEADE/DIESE. 2000. *Pesquisa de Emprego e Desemprego: Indicadores Selecionados.* Sao Paulo: Marzo.

Sen, A. 1989. "Development as Capability Expansion." *Journal of Development Expansion* 19.

_____. 1992. *Inequality Re-examined.* Cambridge, MA: Harvard University Press.

_____. 1999. *Development as Freedom.* New York: Alfred & Knopf.

Serageldin, I. 1998. "The Initiative on Defining, Monitoring and Measuring Social Capital." *Social Capital Initiative Working Paper* No. 1. Washington, DC: The World Bank Social Development Family Environmentally and Socially Sustainable Development Network.

Singh, Anoop, and Charles Collyns. 2005. "Latin America's Resurgence." *Finance and Development* 42 (4), December.

Smith, Stephen. 2005. *Ending Global Poverty: A Guide to What Works.* London: Palgrave Macmillan.

Solow, R. 2000. "Notes on Social Capital and Economic Performance." In Partha Dasgupta and Ismail Serageldin (eds.), *Social Capital: A Multi-Faceted Perspective.* Washington, DC: World Bank.

Stanton-Salazar, R.D., and S.M. Dornbusch. 1995. "Social Capital and the Reproduction of Inequality: Information Networks among Mexican-Origin High School Students." *Sociology of Education* 68.

Stein, Alfredo. 1991. "Las ONG y su rol en el desarrollo social de América Latina." In *La encrucijada de los 90. América Latina en Pensamiento Iberoamericano.* Madrid.

Stiefel, Matthias, and Marshall Wolfe. 1994. *A Voice for the Excluded: Popular Participation in Development: Utopia or Necessity?* London and Atlantic Highlands, NJ: Zed Books and UNRISD.

Stiglitz, J. 2002. *Globalisation and Its Discontents.* New York: Norton Press.

_____. 1998. "More Instruments and Broader Goals: Moving Beyond the Post-Washington Consensus." In *WIDER Annual Lectures,* 2, Helsinki.

Tabb, W.K. 2004. *Economic Governance in the Age of Globalization.* New York: Columbia University Press.

Teachman, J.D., K. Paasch and K. Carver. 1997. "Social Capital and the Generation of Human Capital." *Social Forces* 75 (4).

UNESCO (United Nations Educational, Scientific and Cultural Organisation). 2005. *The World Social Situation: The Inequality Predicament.* New York: UNESCO.

UNCTAD (United Nations Conference on Trade and Development). 2004. "Global investment prospects assessment research note 3: A worldwide survey of the world's largest transnational corporations." *Prospects for FDI Flows, TNC Strategies and Policy Developments: 2004-2007.* New York and Geneva: United Nations <http://www.unctad.org/ sections/dite_dir/docs//survey3> (accessed Dec. 2006).

_____. 2002. *World Investment Report.* New York and Geneva: United Nations.

_____. 1999. *World Investment Report 1999: Foreign Direct Investment and the Challenge of Development.* New York/Geneva: United Nations

UNDP (United Nations Development Programme). 1996, 1999, 2001, 2004. *Human*

Development Report. New York: Oxford University Press.

_____. 1998. "The Global Development Sustainability Facility: 2B2M." *Internal Document*. New York: UNDP.

_____. 1997. *Governance for Sustainable Human Development*. A UNDP Policy Document. New York: UNDP.

_____. 1996. "Good Governance and Sustainable Human Development." Governance Policy Paper. Available at <http://magnet.undp.org/policy> (accessed June 2005).

United Nations. 1998. "The UN and Business: A Global Partnership." Available at <http://www.globalpolicy.org/reform/un-bus.htm> (accessed June 2005).

UNRISD (United Nations Research Institute for Social Development). 2000. "Civil Society Strategies and Movements for Rural Asset Redistribution and Improved Livelihoods," Civil Society and Social Movements Programme. Geneva: UNRISD.

Untoja, F. 1992. *Re-torno al Aullu*. La Paz: CADFA.

Uphof, N. 1994. "Social Capital and Poverty Reduction." In R. Atria et al. (eds.), *Social Capital and Poverty Reduction in Latin America and the Caribbean: Towards a New Paradigm*. Santiago: ECLAC.

Utting, Peter. 2000. "UN-Business Partnerships: Whose Agenda Counts?" *UNRISD News* 23, Autumn-Winter.

Van der Pijl, Kees. 1998. *Transnational Classes and International Relations*. London: Routledge.

Veltmeyer, Henry. 2002. "The Politics of Language: Deconstructing Post-Development Discourse." *Canadian Journal of Development Studies* XX11 (3).

Veltmeyer, Henry, and A.H. O'Malley. 2001. *Transcending Neoliberalism: Community-Based Development*. West Hartford, CT: Kumarian Press.

Veltmeyer, Henry, and James Petras. 1997. *Economic Liberalism and Class Conflict in Latin America*. London: MacMillan Press.

von Gleich, Albrecht. 1999. "Poverty Reduction Strategies: The Experience of Bolivia." In Raundi Halvorson-Quevedo and Hartmut Schneider (eds.), *Waging the Global War on Poverty: Strategies and Case Studies*. Paris: OECD-Development Centre.

Wall, E., G. Ferrazzi and F. Schryer. 1998. "Getting the Goods on Social Capital." *Rural Sociology* 63 (2).

Wallace, Tina. 2003. "NGO Dilemmas: Trojan Horses for Global Neoliberalism?" *Socialist Register 2004*. London: Merlin Press.

Wallace, Tina, Sarah Crowther and Andrew Shephard. 1997. *Standardising Development: Influences on UK NGOs Policies and Procedures*. Oxford: Westview Press.

Weber, Heloise. 2002. "Global Governance and Poverty Reduction: The Case of Microcredit." In Rorden Wilkinson and Steve Hughes (eds.), *Global Governance: Critical Perspectives*. London and New York: Routledge.

Weisbrot, Mark, Dean Baker, Egor Kraev and Judy Chen. 2001. "The Scorecard on Globalization 1980–2000: Twenty Years of Diminished Progress." *Center for Economic and Policy Research* (CEPR), July 11.

White, H., and E. Anderson. 2001. "Growth versus Distribution." Mimeo. Brighton: Institute of Development Studies.

Williamson, John (ed.). 1990. *Latin American Adjustment. How Much Has Happened?*

Washington, DC: Institute for International Economics.

Woolcock, M. 1988. "Social Capital and Economic Development: Towards a Theoretical Synthesis and Policy Framework." *Theory and Society* 27.

_____. 1999. "Managing Risk, Shocks, and Opportunity in Developing Economies: The Role of Social Capital." Available at <www.worldbank.org/poverty/socialcapital>.

_____. 2000. "The Place of Social Capital in Understanding Social and Economic Outcomes." Paper prepared for an International Symposium on the Contribution of Human and Social Capital to Sustained Economic Growth and Well-Being. Quebec City, March 19–21.

Woolcock M., and D. Narayan. 2000. "Social Capital: Implications for Development Theory, Research and Policy." *World Bank Research Observer* 15 (2) August.

World Bank. 1988. *Inequality, Poverty and Growth*. Washington, DC: World Bank.

_____. 1989. *Sub-Saharan Africa: from Crisis to Sustainable Growth*. Washington, DC: World Bank.

_____. 1994. *Governance. The World Bank Experience*. Washington, DC: World Bank.

_____. 1996. *Including the Excluded: Ethnodevelopment in Latin America. Vol. 1*. Washington, DC: World Bank.

_____. 1998. *Assessing Aid. What Works, What Doesn't, and Why*. New York: Oxford University Press.

_____. 1999. *QAG Review Report: Social Development*. Washington, DC: World Bank, Quality Assessment Group.

_____. 2000. *World Development Report: Attacking Poverty*. New York: Oxford University Press.

_____. 2001. *Engendering Development: Through Gender Equality Rights, Resources, and Voice*. New York: Oxford University Press.

_____. 2002. *Reaching the Rural Poor: A Rural Development Strategy for Latin America and the Caribbean*. Washington, DC: World Bank.

_____. 2004a. *Operationalizing Pro-Poor Growth*. Washington, DC: World Bank.

_____. 2004b. *Partnerships in Development: Progress in the Fight against Poverty*. Washington, DC: World Bank.

_____. 2006. "Main Figures—Poverty Reduction and Growth Virtuous and Vicious Circles." Office of the Chief Economist. Available at

Index